Jewish Tales
of
Mystic Joy

Jewish Tales
of
Mystic Joy

Yitzhak Buxbaum

JOSSEY-BASS
A Wiley Company
www.josseybass.com

Published by

 JOSSEY-BASS
A Wiley Company
989 Market Street
San Francisco, CA 94103-1741

www.josseybass.com

Jossey-Bass books and products are available through most bookstores. To
contact Jossey-Bass directly, call (888) 378-2537, fax to (800) 605-2665, or visit
our website at www.josseybass.com.

Substantial discounts on bulk quantities of Jossey-Bass books are available to
corporations, professional associations, and other organizations. For details
and discount information, contact the special sales department at Jossey-Bass.

We at Jossey-Bass strive to use the most environmentally sensitive paper stocks available to us. Our publications are printed on acid-free recycled stock whenever possible, and our paper always meets or exceeds minimum GPO and EPA requirements.

Jossey-Bass also publishes its books in a variety of electronic formats. Some content
that appears in print may not be available in electronic books.

Design by Paula Goldstein.

Library of Congress Cataloging-in-Publication Data

Jewish tales of mystic joy / Yitzhak Buxbaum.— 1st ed.
    p. cm.
ISBN 0-7879-6272-4
1. Joy—Religious aspects—Judaism. 2. Hasidism. 3. Spiritual life—Judaism. I. Title.
BM645.J67 B89 2002
296.1'9—dc21   2002003808

FIRST EDITION
HB Printing 10 9 8 7 6 5 4 3 2 1

Contents

The Tales   19

How Joy and Love Can Conquer Hate 95

Portraits in the Ecstasy of Joy 108

How to Be Joyful 136

This book is dedicated to
Rabbi Shlomo Carlebach
and to all Jews who show their fellow Jews
how joyful Judaism can be.

S'micha
as a Maggid

When my spiritual master, the holy and pure Rabbi Shlomo Carlebach, gave me s'micha (ordination) as a *maggid*, a teller of sacred Jewish tales, he put his holy hands on my head and said:

B'ezrat HaShem
Maggid devarav l'Yaakov.
Aileh hadevarim asher tidabeir el bnai Yisrael.
Bizeh anu somchim v'tomchim u'm'chazkim yidei
Reb Yitzhak ben Meir Buxbaum
sh'yichyeh lihiyot machzir al hap'tachim, pitchaihem
    mikuvanim
petach habayit sha'arei halev liban shel Yisrael
l'hachzir otam avaida mida'at da'at Elyon
b'divrei aggada sh'moshchim liban shel Yisrael
b'divrei hitorerut.
Kumi ori ki va oraich.
Yagid yagid
Y'orair y'orair
Yachzir yachzir
am Yisrael b'tshuvah shleima mitoch ahavah.
Koh t'varchu v'yizkeh lirot b'haramat keren Yisrael mitoch
    simcha.

With the help of God,

Be a *maggid,* a teller of tales, and speak sacred words to
the seed of Jacob.

These are the words you shall speak to the Children of
Israel.

With this, we support, strengthen, and uphold the hands of
Reb Yitzhak son of Meir Buxbaum

To live a life of the spirit, making the rounds, knocking on
all doors, the doors facing each other, the door of the
Temple, the gates of the heart, the Heart of Israel

To return those who are lost, lost to mind,

the Mind of the Most High,

With stories that draw the heart of Israel and cause them to
awaken.

Arise, shine, for your light has come!

Tell, tell

Awaken, awaken

Return, return the People of Israel in complete repentance,
from love.

So shall you bless, and merit to see the raising of the honor
of Israel, in joy.

Acknowledgments

I would like to gratefully acknowledge the help of friends who read the manuscript of this work and offered valuable suggestions to improve its composition and clarity: Matthew Brown, Rachel Ravitz, Fran DeLott, Justin Lewis, Alec Gelcer, Chana-Chaya Bailey, and my friend and editor, Alan Rinzler. I am grateful also to Rabbi Meir Fund of Brooklyn, who was always ready to provide information or advice when needed about any Jewish topic.

Introduction

There are many Jewish tales that vividly show the joy, bliss, and ecstasy of holy people, particularly the *tzaddikim,* the Hasidic movement's charismatic leaders, and the Hasidim, their devoted followers. This book contains a selection of these tales that portray the mystic joy that comes from a passionate love for God.

The Jewish mystics say that the ultimate human aim is to attain the bliss that God intends for us. For that reason, we need to read and hear tales about mystic joy, to see the happiness that awaits us if we strive for holiness. The Hasidic stories draw us into the world of the tales and allow us to taste the mystic joy the tales describe. I hope that reading these enchanting sacred stories gives you holy pleasure and that their sweetness inspires you to seek mystic happiness and joy for yourself.

MYSTIC JOY

To fully appreciate the tales, we must understand the teachings of the Rabbis about mystic joy, about ecstasy and bliss.

According to Jewish mystic teaching, God's presence, the *Shechinah* ("Indwelling"), is everywhere, and there is no place where God is not present. One of the main goals of Jewish mystics is to go beyond mere belief and observance to attain spiritual experience, acting and meditating so as to achieve *d'vekut,* a constant loving awareness of the Divine Presence. That is the essence of mysticism—directly knowing God.

D'vekut, say the mystics, brings with it intense spiritual delight, for, since God's nature is bliss, the essence of God-awareness is bliss. They often quote the Torah verse "There is strength and gladness in His place"[1]—saying that if one reaches God's place, one will share in His bliss, for nearness to God produces mystic joy and ecstasy.

An ancient rabbinic parable tells of a princess who married a very wealthy commoner. Eager to please his wife and make her happy, the man gave her everything a devoted husband could give his wife—a gorgeous mansion with the finest, most expensive furniture; an exquisite wardrobe; many personal servants to attend to her every need.

Yet he saw that she was unmoved by everything that he gave her and asked her about it.

She explained to him that no matter *what* he gave her, she had had better in her father's palace.[2]

The Rabbis say that the "princess" is the soul that has descended to this world from heaven, and the parable teaches that no matter what a person attains materially in this world—money, a good job, a wonderful spouse and family—his soul will never be made happy by worldly things but only by spiritual things, for the soul is a "princess" from a higher realm.

According to Jewish mystic teaching, the soul is an actual part of God. Therefore, its essential nature is bliss and joy. The soul yearns for joy; it requires joy; but it can only be satisfied with spiritual joys and pleasures that reveal and disclose its true nature.

Why did God, who is perfect and needs nothing, create the world? The Jewish mystics say He created the world in order to share

His supreme bliss with creatures, with human beings. How, then, can a person attain this exalted state, reveal his innate potential, and share the divine bliss and joy? Only by cleaving to God in devotion, fulfilling His will, and delighting in divine providence.

All worldly happiness is ephemeral and susceptible to change, since it depends on a cause. When the cause disappears, so too does the happiness. Worldly success may disappear in an instant. Everyone knows about famous individuals—politicians, business magnates, celebrities—who fell from the heights of success to the depths of failure and humiliation. The Rabbis say there is a "wheel" in the world; someone on top today may be on the bottom tomorrow. Even if a person has arranged a wonderful life for himself, with family and work, with everything in its proper place, unexpected events can suddenly destroy his worldly happiness; the matter is out of his control.

One can never find permanent happiness in impermanent pleasures. Only divine joy is eternal and unchanging, because it manifests and reveals the inner truth of the human soul. All the enjoyments a person derives from external objects and worldly pleasures cannot compare to the immense joy that lies within us, if we can only tap it, if we can only contact our soul and its heavenly source of unlimited joy. When a person cleaves in devotion to the Divine Presence and shares in divine bliss, his joy is constant and immune to any worldly change. Who would not want that? Indeed, deep down, that is what everyone wants—unending, unchanging, unceasing joy.[3]

MYSTICAL AND JOYFUL HASIDISM

Most of the stories in this collection are Hasidic, which is no accident, since Hasidism actively fosters and encourages religious joy. Let us briefly consider the connection between Hasidic mysticism and joy.

Hasidism, which began as a pietistic revival movement in eighteenth-century Eastern Europe, founded by Rabbi Yisrael Baal Shem Tov, represents a living Jewish mystic tradition. Part of what made it different from the Judaism of its time is that it was both

mystical and joyful, with an emphasis on love of God and uninhib-
ited devotion. The religious establishment of rabbis and scholars,
however, emphasized the fear and awe of God. They tended toward
strictness and severity and an accompanying sadness. In fact, the
terrible antisemitism of the period had produced a sadness and depression among Jews that had infiltrated even Jewish religious life,
giving rise to an ascetic and morose form of piety.

Rabbi Yisrael Baal Shem Tov broke this spiritual bondage to
sadness and misery and restored the Torah path of love of God and
joy. One reason he was able to inspire a vibrant new religious reform
movement is that he was a mystic who realized in his own life the
abundant spiritual blessings promised by the ancient Jewish mystic
tradition to those who achieve the goal of God-consciousness. He
had reached God's place of bliss and joy and could lead others there.

The Baal Shem Tov ("Master of Divine Names") taught his new
mystic path to the spiritually inclined among the religious elite, but
he also reached out to the common folk. Many of the contemporary
rabbis, who focused exclusively on the intricacies of talmudic scholarship and on an exacting observance of Jewish religious law, looked
down on the often unlearned and imperfectly observant Jewish
masses. Because the Baal Shem Tov cherished the common people's simple faith and devoted loyalty to Judaism and communicated
to them his loving appreciation, large numbers of them flocked to
Hasidism's banner, and the new movement expanded rapidly.

Another prominent innovation of the early Hasidic movement
was its strongly communal orientation. Hasidic religious communities
were organized around charismatic mystics called *tzaddikim* (plural
of *tzaddik*) or *rebbes*. Most people could not be full-blown mystics,
but they could still be close to God by attaching themselves to true
mystics, such as the Baal Shem Tov and his disciples, who would lead
them to God and to the joy that comes from His nearness.

Early Hasidism produced a wealth of tales about the tzaddikim.
Storytelling about them was viewed as a sacred act that inspired people to attach themselves to the rebbes and to imitate their holy ways.

These tales described the rebbes' holiness and kindness, their mystic attachment to God, and also their ecstatic joy.

THE RELATIONSHIP BETWEEN
MYSTICISM AND JOY

The Baal Shem Tov taught that God is everywhere and always near, and a person who cleaves to Him through that fervent belief will experience His nearness and be filled with joy.[4] He also taught that to make spiritual progress and achieve mystic states of consciousness, a person must be joyful. According to Jewish mystic teaching, since both God-awareness and joy are states of expanded consciousness, they naturally belong together and mutually affect each other. The Hasidic rebbes said that a person who is God-conscious becomes joyful, and a person who is joyful, even because of worldly joys and pleasures, draws closer to God. The mystics actually see divinity; they see that all the world and everything in it is alive with Godliness. Joy opens a person's eyes to this awesome and thrilling God-vision. Joy has tremendous spiritual power.[5] If even worldly joy can bring a person closer to God, how much more is that true of spiritual joy! The Holy Ari, the great medieval kabbalist, revealed that he reached his exalted mystic level only because of the joy with which he performed the *mitzvot*, the Torah's divine commandments.

TRACING JOY TO ITS SOURCE

Rebbe Nachman of Bratzlav, the great-grandson of the Baal Shem Tov and a great Hasidic mystic, told the following parable:

≈◈≈ A man went to a wedding and walked around listening to what the guests were saying. He overheard some people saying, "Oh, the food here is terrific! I haven't eaten such good food in a long time!"

He thought, "They're not really at a wedding. They're at a restaurant."

Then he overheard some people saying, "It's so nice to see old friends and family. And the music's unbelievable!"

He thought, "They're at a party."

Then he overheard some people saying, "Isn't it wonderful that Moshe and Shprintza are getting married?"

"Ah," he thought, "they're at a wedding!"

After the feast, he went for a walk in the woods behind the wedding hall and reflected on his experience.

Finally, he looked up and said, "God in heaven, thank You so much for all the weddings in the world, that two people can join in love and become one!"

He walked on a while farther, then looked up and said, "God, thank You for all the joy in the world!"[6] ∞

Weddings and the joining together of soulmates are the most intense expression of the joy that God gives to the world.

The kabbalists teach that all joy, all pleasure comes from God; it is a revelation of His *Shechinah,* His Divine Presence in this world. But joy and pleasure can be experienced on many different levels, higher and lower, one above the other. A person can enjoy merely the physical and sensual taste of food, or he can realize that the taste itself is Godliness and a manifestation of God's closeness. The mystic path traces all pleasure and joy back to its single divine root. A mystic finds at the end that all earthly and bodily pleasures have their source in God, and he experiences all of life as a revelation of the one divine reality, a reality that is nothing other than an expression of bliss and joy.

JOY IN HIS PLACE

The Torah verse that says there is "gladness in His place" teaches that if one reaches God's place, one will share His bliss. When a person begins the Jewish spiritual journey, he thinks that to reach God's place, he must find holiness in a synagogue or near a holy teacher. And that is true. But eventually he realizes the deeper mystical truth. The Rabbis teach that "God is the Place of the world."[7] One of the traditional names for God is "the Place."[8] The Baal Shem Tov described the relation between God and the world as like a snail whose shell-home is part of its own being. Therefore, one is always in God's place, for God dwells within the world, which is also divine. And since God is bliss, all the world that emanates from Him is bliss. A mystic realizes that there is nothing but Him and nothing but joy and bliss in everything that happens. All events—the good and the seemingly bad—are like waves of joy passing through the one Reality. Our very being is also part of that blissful Reality, and everything we experience, whether happy or sad, is in essence ecstasy and bliss, if we only seek our inner root.

JOY ABOVE AND BELOW

One way the Baal Shem Tov and the rebbes who followed him tried to shake the Jewish people out of their depression and melancholy was by teaching them that God wanted them to be happy. In fact, they said, if a person believes in God, he *must* be happy, for God is all good and everything He does is good. Sadness shows that one does not really believe this. To put it radically, sadness is a sign of atheism.

Rabbi Dov Ber, the Maggid (preacher) of Mezritch, the Baal Shem Tov's great disciple and his successor as leader of the Hasidic movement, taught that the "face above" reflects the face below. God's face toward you reflects your face. If your face is sad, so is God's face to you; but if your face is joyful, so is God's face.[9] Sadness draws to you unhappy events; joy draws to you God's blessings.

The *Zohar*, the central book of the Kabbalah, says:

Come and see! The lower world is always waiting to receive and it is called "the jewel." And the upper world bestows [its light, which is reflected in the jewel] only according to the receptivity of the lower world. If your face shines with joy below, then Heaven [God] shines to you from above, but if there is sadness below, Heaven dispenses judgment. Therefore, serve God with joy, because a person's joy draws to him joy from above."[10]

If you are joyful, Heaven sends you blessings and adds joy to your joy.

LOVING JOY AND HATING SADNESS

According to Kabbalah, the worlds below reflect the worlds above. The mystic teaching that God's face shines with joy at a person who is joyful expresses itself in this lower world in the common fact that everyone loves a happy person. In a profound but provocative insight, some Hasidic rebbes claimed that God finds a joyful person so irresistibly appealing that He cannot refuse even a joyful sinner entrance into His presence.

⫷ There was a man in Lublin who was a notable sinner yet was granted an audience whenever he wanted to speak with Rebbe Yaakov Yitzhak, the holy Seer of Lublin, as if he were among the rebbe's inner circle. Hundreds and sometimes thousands of people came to visit the Seer at one time. Others who were less privileged than this man had to wait days, weeks, or even months to see the rebbe.

Some of the Hasidim were irritated by the favor shown to this man and complained among themselves, "Is it possible our master does not know that this per-

son is a great sinner? If the rebbe knew, he would certainly not be so friendly with him!"

When they told the Seer, he answered apologeti-
cally, saying, "I know about him as well as you. But
what can I do? I love happiness and hate sadness! And
he is such a confirmed sinner that even though most
sinners momentarily regret their act afterward—which
does not stop them, however, from going back to their
sinning later—this man does not regret his sins the
least bit and he is not sad for even a moment! I find his
happiness so appealing that I cannot keep from talking
with him!"[11] ❧

The Seer of Lublin's attitude reflected the attitude of God. Just as even
a sinner's joy gains him entrance into God's presence, depression
blocks the divine light and keeps a person from approaching God.
The ancient rabbis expounded the Torah verse "There is strength and
gladness in His place" by saying that one may not enter the gates to
the king's palace wearing a mourner's sackcloth.[12] Rebbe Yisrael of
Rizhin, who, like the Seer of Lublin, loved joy and happiness and
hated sadness and depression, reflected this "etiquette" of the divine palace. A morose Hasid, who always wept when praying and
walked around with a glum expression on his face, who mistakenly
thought that a pious person must be miserable and melancholy, was
not allowed into the rebbe's presence. "He is drawing nourishment
from the unclean side," the rebbe would say.[13] If that Hasid wanted
to be near the rebbe, he had to change his ways, abandon his misguided piety, and at least try to be happy!

The Rizhiner taught his Hasidim, "A Jew who wants to cleave
to God, blessed be He, about whom it is said, 'strength and gladness
are in His place,' cannot allow himself to become sad. If a Jew has forgotten to be happy, it is a sign that, God forbid, he has forgotten God.
I must tell you," he continued, "that I suspect that many nonreligious

assimilated Jews will attain the World to Come in the merit of their un-failing happiness."[14] Thus a happy sinner was permitted to enter the rebbe's presence, but a morose Hasid was excluded!

It is, however, important to distinguish between two kinds of sadness. Whereas depression makes a person melancholy and closes him to other people and to God, the rebbes teach that the sadness of repentance—a person's bitterness and heartbrokenness over his spiritual failures—eventually opens him to God and to people. In the end, such holy sadness always enlivens a person and leads to joy.

A person may enjoy many different kinds of pleasure in life. Each individual must choose which pleasures to enjoy, which of them to seek and focus on—the lower and lesser worldly pleasures or the higher and greater spiritual pleasures. The happy sinner to whom the Lubliner was attracted and the nonreligious people mentioned by the Rizhiner are certainly not the Jewish ideal! As the tales in this book reveal, the greatest worldly happiness, even if unblemished by regrets, pales beside the radiant mystic joy of those who have drawn close to the living God.

Religion not only *should* be joyful, it *must* be. A person who does not derive joy from his religious involvement will not progress spiritually. The Baal Shem Tov taught that the soul, whose source and root is in the World of Joy, requires joy by its very nature. Someone who deprives himself of the higher holy joy will be forced to seek and enjoy only lower worldly and bodily pleasures that are ultimately unsatisfying.[15]

The Baal Shem Tov, the Lubliner, the Rizhiner, and other rebbes taught that a religious person should avoid sadness at all costs. One could almost say they taught that sadness is forbidden! But their intention was not to make unhappy people doubly sad by telling them that they were also sinning! Their happy teaching "prohibiting" sadness should make a person smile! God so much wants you to be happy and joyful that He positively forbids you to be sad! This lesson can be a potent stimulus to joy. The whole point of the rebbes' charmingly provocative teaching is for a person to use the powerful notion that sadness is actually forbidden to wrench himself out of depressed states of mind and seek happiness. Where? In God's presence!

GOD IS WITH US

We must not be unsubtle in appreciating Hasidic teachings about joy. The divine "command" to be joyful does not mean that a truly religious person will always walk around with a smiling, happy face, like a fool. But we should make our sad times short, taste the bitterness God has given us, and return to happiness in God's presence. The goal is to be happy, but when a person is sad and heartbroken, God, and also a tzaddik, will console him. Even a mystic can be sad—as Ecclesiastes states about the human condition: "There is a time to weep and a time to laugh, a time to mourn and a time to dance."[16] There are times for holy sadness and anguish, such as when a person laments his faults or shares the sufferings of others or even the suffering of the Divine Presence, for the Rabbis tell us that God suffers when people suffer, and the pious willingly share in that divine suffering too. But a true mystic will even in sadness experience, at a deeper level of awareness, ecstasy and bliss at his closeness to God.

A Hasidic story casts light on this perspective.

≈⟨⟩ Rabbi Moshe Teitelbaum, who later became the Oheler Rebbe, was at first not a Hasid. He was attracted to the Hasidim in his town, but he had one important question about their conduct, which seemed to contradict the *Shulhan Aruch,* the Code of Jewish Law. The Hasidic way is to always rejoice, but is it not explicitly stated in the *Shulhan Aruch* that a pious person should be constantly troubled and anguished about the destruction of the holy Temple? If so, thought Rabbi Moshe, why are the Hasidim always rejoicing?[17] His objection to what seemed to him to be excessive Hasidic joy caused him to stay away from the Hasidim, although, otherwise, their ways pleased him and he was attracted to them.

When Rabbi Moshe arranged for his daughter to marry a young Torah scholar who happened to be a Hasid, he demanded as part of the written conditions for the marriage that the young man leave the Hasidic movement. The young man said he would do so if Rabbi Moshe agreed to one condition that he, the groom, would set, namely, that Rabbi Moshe visit the Seer of Lublin at least once, to see the Hasidim for himself at first hand and by questioning the Seer attempt to have his doubts about them removed. The deal was made. The young son-in-law-to-be was certain that once Rabbi Moshe saw the awesomely holy Seer of Lublin, his doubts would disappear and the Seer would answer any questions he might pose.

And that was what happened. When he went to visit the Seer, as he had agreed with his future son-in-law, he prayed, "O God, You know my thoughts and my heart and know that I have no desire to question any of Your ways. Be with me then and help me when I visit this holy tzaddik so that he will answer this question I have, because our Sages have said that 'when a person comes to purify himself, they help him.'[18] It doesn't say 'He' in the singular—which would mean that God alone helps him—but 'they' in the plural—meaning [the rabbi interprets] that people help him too. So let this tzaddik be one of those who help me find the truth."

As soon as Rabbi Moshe entered the Seer's presence, before he had spoken a word, the Seer mystically read his thoughts and asked him, "Why do you look so sad? It's true that it's written in the *Shulhan Aruch* that a pious person should be troubled and anxious about the destruction of the Temple, but a person can fulfill this, mourn for the Temple, and still be joyful.[19] Believe me when I tell you that every night we recite the Midnight Lamentation over the destruction of the Temple with weeping and mourning, but it is still all with joy, for that is what my holy master and teacher, Rebbe Shmelke of Nikolsburg, taught us with a parable:

"There was a king who was captured in a war and exiled to a distant land. Once, he went to visit the house of one of his devoted subjects who was also in that country. Now when this man saw his beloved king in exile, he went away and wept without restraint. But with all that, he rejoiced, because his king was lodging with him. The parable's application is easily understood," said the Seer of Lublin to Rabbi Moshe, "*for the* Shechinah, *the Divine Presence, is with us,* and although one must not speak too openly about such things, as it is written, 'Walk modestly with the Lord your God'—that is, if God is with you, be modest and do not proclaim it openly—yet the Sages have also said, 'When someone comes to purify himself, they help him'—it does not say 'He' helps but 'they' help, so we too must help you." ✦

A non-Hasidic rabbi also answered the question that troubled Rabbi Moshe Teitelbaum.

✦ Rabbi Avraham Yeshaya Karelitz, the Hazon Ish,[20] was always joyful, even when he discussed matters that deserved tears. When his students, in surprise, questioned him, wondering "How can it be?" he replied, with his face shining, "The prophet Jeremiah composed the scroll of Lamentations over the destruction of the Temple. When he wrote 'Weep, O weep in the night,' he undoubtedly wept. He shed tears over the destruction of 'the daughter of his people.' But there seems to be a contradiction here. The prophet wrote this with the holy spirit, yet the Rabbis tell us that the holy spirit rests only on someone who is joyful. The answer is that it is possible to weep bitterly about the destruction of the Temple and at the same time to be joyful."[21] ≈⬦≈

JOY AND JUDAISM

The Hasidic rebbes teach that joy and Judaism should be synonymous. Why is knowing about Judaism's mystic joy so important today? Because many people mistakenly think of religion as a deadening burden of dos and don'ts, of countless rules, restrictions, and regulations. And there are religious people whose faulty, mistaken conception of piety gives others this wrong impression. But this is an old story. The Hasidic rebbes have always taught that those "pious" people who heap on restrictions that stifle joy and happiness are actually perverting religion. Whether they call themselves "Hasidim" or not, their attitude is the *opposite* of real Hasidism and real Hasidic piety.[22]

The true purpose of religious limitations on worldliness is only to release the soul for its free flight into the spiritual realms of holy joy. Adam and Eve's mistake was in failing to realize that by obeying God's command, by restricting their physical pleasure and avoiding eating from just one tree among the many permissible, they would open themselves up to more intense and fulfilling spiritual pleasures and would enjoy the eternal bliss and delight of the Garden of Eden.

Rabbi Yaakov Kranz, the Maggid of Dubnow, the most famous
Jewish preacher of the eighteenth century, told the following parable.

☙ A jewelry merchant and a tool seller, traveling
separately on business, checked into the same hotel in
a certain town at the same time. The jewelry merchant
had with him his small suitcase, containing his diamonds, pearls, and other jewels; the other merchant
had a big, heavy trunk containing hammers, saws, and
all kinds of work tools.

The jewelry merchant asked a porter to take his
suitcase up to his room. The porter came down soon
afterward and presented himself for a tip, and the merchant gave him something. But instead of leaving, the
porter coughed and shrugged and made it clear that
he was not satisfied with the tip. He mumbled that the
suitcase was "so heavy" and so difficult to "drag up
the stairs."

The surprised merchant said to him, "If you're
talking about a heavy suitcase and how hard it was to
drag up the stairs, you've made a mistake! That was not
my suitcase! *My* suitcase is very light! You took the
wrong suitcase!" ☙

The Maggid of Dubnow said that this is the situation with Judaism:
If someone finds his involvement with Jewish practices and customs
burdensome and heavy, he has made a mistake. It's the wrong suitcase! Judaism's purpose is to *enliven* a person and make him *happier*. If it is dull and deadening, that is not the real Judaism!—for
Judaism is about joy.

ABOUT THE TALES

Many of the tales in this book are newly translated from Hebrew. Some were heard orally and are appearing in print for the first time. Others have been retold. They are arranged into sections for the reader's convenience; many of them would have fit quite easily into any of several sections. There is a certain relaxed logic to the sequence of the tales and sections that perhaps the reader will sense. The purpose of religious tales cannot be fulfilled if they cannot be understood. To help readers more fully appreciate the tales, I have placed before some sections a preface explaining Jewish concepts or terms contained in the stories of that section. After the tales, I have occasionally offered some commentary. Readers unfamiliar with Jewish religious terms can also use the Glossary at the back of the book.

All the tales in this book are about Hasidic rebbes and Hasidim, with the exception of the following:

> *"God Is with Us"—Rabbi Avraham Yeshaya Karelitz, the*
> *Hazon Ish (p. 11)*
> *"The Bach's Partner in Heaven"—Rabbi Yoel Sirkes, the*
> *Bach (p. 44)*
> *"The Dance of Parting"—Rabbi Yisrael Meir of Radin, the*
> *Hafetz Hayim; Rabbi Elhanan Wasserman (p. 158)*
> *"The Dance of Holy Friendship"—Rabbi Avraham Yeshaya*
> *Karelitz, the Hazon Ish (p. 161)*
> *"Dancing with God"—whether Hasidic or not is unknown*
> *(p. 162)*
> *"Revived by a Song"—Rabbi Mordechai Yaffeh (p. 185)*
> *"Reb Arele's* Sukkot*"—whether Hasidic or not is unknown*
> *(p. 192)*
> *"Joy Until the Final Moment of Life"—Rabbi Meir Shapiro*
> *(p. 206)*

Note that the title *Rebbe* before a name always indicates a rabbi who is a Hasidic leader. However, when a story seems to be about a rebbe at a period in his life before he became a leader, I have used the title *Rabbi*. In popular usage, a non-Hasidic rabbi may also occasionally be called "rebbe" as a title of respect, meaning "revered teacher," but it would not be used before his name. *Reb* is an honorific title, meaning something like "Mister," used with a person's first name—for example, Reb Moshe.

A number of the tales mention specific songs. When telling these stories, one can try to find and use melodies for those verses.

The Tales

Rabbi Yisrael Baal Shem Tov

The Baal Shem Tov taught that a Jew should always be joyful, believing with complete faith that the Divine Presence is always with him. The Besht himself was a true mystic, who lived immersed in divine joy. (*Besht* is an acronym for Baal Shem Tov.)

How can a person attain mystic joy? Knowing that God is near brings joy. The Besht taught that everything in the world is God and God is everything;[1] he also said that a Jew should believe with total faith that God is with him, by him, near him.[2] He should strive to perceive God's presence everywhere and realize that all that he hears, sees, and experiences is divinity, that God's glory fills the earth and there is no place where He is not present. A Jew should especially perceive Godliness in the Torah's teachings and fuse his soul with the soul of the Torah. The Baal Shem Tov shared and taught the kabbalistic view that God, the Jewish people, and the Torah are one mystic unity, the Torah joining each Jew in a mystic bond with God. To the extent that a Jew unites himself with the Torah—so that God's thoughts becomes his thoughts, God's heart becomes his heart, and God's ways become his ways—he will share in the divine bliss and joy.

The Besht made mysticism accessible to common people, so that even nonmystics could taste mystic happiness. By fervently believing in God's nearness and goodness, a person will come to feel God's intimate presence in his life. This leads to mystic joy, even amid troubles and suffering—but only if one chooses a pious perspective of faith and trust in God.

Knowing the mystic joy of God's nearness, the Besht brought singing and dancing to the center of Hasidic life. Since music produces an ecstatic revelation of the soul, mysticism and music are natural partners. The Talmud says, "Which kind of worship especially involves joy and happiness?—song."³ The Baal Shem Tov sang as a form of worship, and he opened the gates of the path of music for his disciples and followers. "By means of music," he told them, "you can attain joy and *d'vekut* with the Infinite One, blessed be He."⁴ The Besht also danced in worship and inspired his disciples to dance, saying, "The purpose of holy dancing is to ascend spiritually and to reveal the divinity of all reality."⁵

The Baal Shem Tov taught that there is another benefit to joyful prayer, to singing and dancing in worship, for the joy of devotion sweetens (ameliorates) heavenly decrees: the face above reflects the face below. But not all sadness is forbidden. The Baal Shem Tov knew the ecstasy of weeping and mourning too.

The Baal Shem Tov's Parable of the Fiddler

⋘ The fervent singing and dancing of the Baal Shem Tov's disciples was frowned on by the drier, more conventional Torah scholars, who criticized what they perceived as his and his disciples' improper conduct. These critics once asked him why his disciples and followers were so excessively joyful and danced so frequently, seemingly at every opportunity. The Besht answered them with a parable, saying:

"Once, a skilled and talented fiddler stood in the street playing in an ecstasy of passion and feeling. A crowd gathered around him to listen, and they were so charmed by the beauty and sweetness of his music that they began to dance, lost to the world.

"A deaf man happened to pass by, and unable to hear the ravishing music, he was utterly astonished by the bizarre scene before his eyes. Since he could not fathom why the people were dancing, he was certain that they were actually madmen!

"That is the way it is with my disciples and followers," said the Baal Shem Tov. "They hear and see the song that emanates from each and every thing that God, blessed be He, has created. If so, how can they keep from dancing?"[6] ❧

The Kabbalah teaches that the whole universe reverberates with the music of divinity. Each creation and creature "sings" its joyful testimony of its Creator. The famous kabbalistic Book of Song, *Perek Shira,* says that all creatures, both animals and plants, sing praises to their Creator. The calls and cries of the many different kinds of animals—the lowing of cows, the cackling of hens, the croaking of frogs—are all songs praising God. Even inanimate creations, such as stones, sing wordless songs of devotion to the One and Only One. If only—like the Baal Shem Tov and his disciples—we had the ears to hear!

The Baal Shem Tov Dances with the Spiritual Torah

Jewish mystics teach that when God's Word descended from heaven, it split in two: one part created the world, and the other part became the Torah. The mystics see divine revelation both in the creation and in the Torah.

On the holiday of *Simhat Torah* (Joy of the Torah), Jews sing and dance in the synagogue with all the Torah scrolls to celebrate God's gift of His Word to the Jewish people. Rabbi Menachem Mendel Schneersohn, the late Lubavitcher Rebbe, taught, "You must always be joyful, as the Torah says, 'Serve God with joy'—just as the 'serve God' must be always, so too must the 'with joy' be always. Nevertheless, we must be especially joyful on holidays, which are the special times for joy; and most especially on Simhat Torah, for then our joy must be unlimited."[7]

One Simhat Torah night, the Baal Shem Tov danced ecstatically, in the midst of his holy disciples, as he clasped a Torah scroll to his breast. After handing the Torah to one of his disciples, he continued to dance without it.

Rabbi Yitzhak, another disciple, saw this and said, "Our holy master has now handed over the physical Torah and has taken to himself the spiritual Torah."

Later, when the Baal Shem Tov heard this comment repeated, he said, "I'm surprised that Rabbi Yitzhak is on the level to see such things!"[8]

Rebbe Leib Saras, a disciple of the Maggid of Mezritch, taught that a Jew must absorb the Torah so deeply into himself that he *becomes* a Torah.[9] When he achieves that, he can act according to his heart's desire, and every move he makes, every step he takes, will be directed by God.

Heikel the Water Carrier

When asked, in casual conversation, "How are you?" pious Jews traditionally respond, "*Baruch HaShem!*" ("Praise God!"), for regardless of what is happening in a person's life, he should believe that it is for the good and praise God. Some pious people never complain about anything that happens to them, considering that to do so would show a lack of faith and trust in God's goodness. The Baal Shem Tov taught that a total belief in divine providence is the secret of happiness and contentment.

≈≈≈ One day, Heikel the Water Carrier passed by the house of the Baal Shem Tov with two pails of water weighing down on his shoulders.

The Besht, who was standing outside on the street with his disciples, asked him, "How are you today, Reb Heikel?"

Heikel, whose face was overcast with a gloomy expression, almost groaned in answering, "I won't lie, Reb Yisrael. I'm not happy. As I'm getting older, my strength is getting less and less every day, and our fellow Jews have invented a new custom: They're building their houses on every hillside and right up to the top! It's hard for me to climb all the way up there with the two heavy buckets on my back. So my livelihood is suffering. I'm not making much of a living these days. May God have mercy!"

The next day, the Besht was with the same disciples outside his house, and again they saw Heikel coming toward them with the two full pails of water loaded on his shoulders. But this time his face shone with a happy glow.

Once again, the Besht asked, "How are you today, Reb Heikel?"

Heikel smiled broadly and in a voice suffused with contentment, replied, "Praise God! Reb Yisrael. God

forbid that I should complain about the Master of the
world. Everything's fine with me! There's nothing a person can't get used to. When I was young, the two full
water buckets weighed down on my back and tired me
out. But when people grow older, they can become used
to anything. Now, thank God, I no longer even feel their
weight. I tell you, they're as light as feathers on my
shoulders. I'm only happy that God still gives me the
strength to do something for my fellow Jews and bring
them the water they need!"

After Heikel left, the Baal Shem Tov turned to his
disciples and said, "Do you see this? The same Heikel,
the same heavy pair of water buckets, the same houses
high up on the hillsides. Yet it's as if there were two different Heikels! Look how different the Heikel of today
is from the Heikel of yesterday!

"When he is dissatisfied, he grumbles and com-
plains and actually feels as if he has no strength left.
But on a day when he is content with his lot, he is blessing and praising the Creator of the world for giving him
the strength to serve people by bringing buckets of
water to their houses.

"The truth is that Heikel must be a water carrier;
that is his lot in life. But it is he who decides every day
whether he will happily labor at his work or, God forbid,
will bitterly drudge away in sadness and misery. Someone might think that today Heikel had a good day and
yesterday a bad day. It's not so.

"*I tell you, there are no good times and bad times;
there are only happy times and sad times. For* every-

thing *that God, blessed be He, does is for good; it all
depends on how we receive it."*[10] ❧

The Parable of the Sweeper

❧ The Baal Shem Tov once arrived in a certain
town before Rosh HaShanah and asked the people:
Who would be leading the prayers during the Days
of Awe?

They replied that it was the rabbi of the town.

"And how does he lead the prayers?" the Besht
asked.

"On Yom Kippur," they said, "he chants the whole
Confession of Sins in a cheerful tune."

The Besht sent for the rabbi and asked him about
his strange custom.

The rabbi replied, "The least and lowliest of the
king's servants, who cleans out the sewers and sweeps
the garbage and filth from the courtyard, is as happy
as can be while he cleans, because he's cleaning the
courtyard of the king, and he sings a cheerful tune as
he sweeps, for his work pleases the king."

"If that's the intention with which you pray," said
the Baal Shem Tov, "may my lot be with yours."

Later the Besht explained to his disciples that
by praying with a happy melody, the rabbi "sweetened
the heavenly judgments"–he ameliorated any heavenly
decree that threatened the community because of its
sins."[11] ❧

His Disciples Dance on the New Moon

⤐ One year, during the Yom Kippur prayers, the Baal
Shem Tov saw with his holy spirit that harm would come
to the Jewish people if he and his disciples did not make
the traditional blessing of the new moon immediately
following the holiday. Then this great *mitzvah* would be
joined to the side of merit and incline the balance of the
scale of judgment to good.

But the new moon was not visible at the end of
Yom Kippur, and the blessing could not be recited. So
the Besht, who was depressed about this, attempted to
use his mystic powers to cause the moon to appear. He
asked his disciples several times to go outside and see
if the moon was visible, but in spite of his great efforts,
the skies remained overcast with dark clouds, and it
seemed unlikely there would be a moon that night.

The Besht's disciples knew nothing about their
master's worries or about the heavenly decree and how
important it was that they bless the moon after Yom
Kippur. It was their custom to celebrate at the end of
Yom Kippur, since they had completed their divine
service successfully, led by their holy master, the Baal
Shem Tov, whose service on Yom Kippur was like that
of the high priest in the ancient Temple. They had full
trust that their prayers were accepted and that they
were signed and sealed for a good year.

So this time too, they were joyously dancing with
holy fervor. At first, they danced in the outer room of
the Besht's house, but afterward, carried on the wave of

their exuberant joy, they burst into their master's room and danced in his presence. When the joy and ecstasy of their dancing surged even more strongly, they dared to draw the Baal Shem Tov himself into their circle. They swept their holy master into their midst, and he began to dance with them.

While they were dancing this sacred dance, those outside suddenly called out loudly that the moon was visible, and they all went out quickly to bless the moon that night.

The Baal Shem Tov then said that what he could not accomplish by his mystic powers, the Hasidim had accomplished by their joy.[12] ⨾⊸⊸

With Joy and with Sadness

The Baal Shem Tov attracted many followers because his deep concern for the welfare of his fellow Jews was obvious. He rejoiced in their good fortune and was saddened by their bad fortune, whether in their material or in their spiritual affairs. His powerful bond of sympathy with others gave him the power to move them by his words and deeds. He could touch people's hearts and turn them to God.

⨾⊸⊸ The first time the Besht visited the town of Slutzk in Lithuania—a bastion of opponents to his new way—he arrived right before *Rosh Hodesh*, the New Moon celebration. In Slutzk, the people followed the custom of observing the day before Rosh Hodesh as a *Yom Kippur Katan*, a Lesser Day of Atonement, a day of fasting and repentance. At noon before Yom Kippur Katan, which began that evening, they announced that all work in town should cease so that everyone—men, women, and children—could come to the synagogue for the afternoon prayers. Following the afternoon and evening prayers, they announced that everyone should return to the synagogue that night for *Tikkun Hatzot,* the Midnight Lamentation Service, and that the following day too would be a day of fasting until the evening and of a cessation from work.

That night, after the Midnight Service, the town preacher delivered a sermon to the people in the synagogue, to arouse them to repent. He took his theme from a puzzling saying of the Sages:

> The purpose of the days is the nights;
> The purpose of the nights is the Sabbaths;
> The purpose of the Sabbaths is the New Moons;
> The purpose of the New Moons is the holidays;
> The purpose of the holidays is Rosh HaShanah;
> The purpose of Rosh HaShanah is Yom Kippur;
> The purpose of Yom Kippur is repentance;
> The purpose of repentance is the World to Come.

The preacher chose this saying because of its connection to their holy task that night—to repent on Yom Kippur Katan before Rosh Hodesh—and he explained it this way:

"'The purpose of the days is the nights' because at night, we have time to study the Torah, as the Rabbis said: 'The night was created for study.' 'The purpose of the nights is the Sabbaths' because on the Sabbath, we are completely free from work and can dedicate ourselves to Torah study for the whole day, not just at night.

'The purpose of the Sabbaths is the New Moons' because on Rosh Hodesh, life for that month is decreed in heaven, and life is given to us to study the Torah. 'The purpose of the New Moons is the holidays' because, as is known, a special heavenly light is revealed during a holiday that illuminates our Torah study. 'The purpose of the holidays is Rosh HaShanah' because on Rosh HaShanah, light and life for the whole year descend to us from heaven. 'The purpose of Rosh HaShanah is Yom Kippur' because on Yom Kippur, we are detached from all worldly concerns and are like angels. 'The purpose of Yom Kippur is repentance'—is self-evident. 'The purpose of repentance is the World to Come' because by repentance, we gain the World to Come."

The preacher expounded each part of the saying at length, explaining it according to his understanding, as best he could. And the whole congregation—of men, women, and children—were aroused by his words, and they all began to sob as they wept in repentance.

After the preacher's sermon, he and everyone else went home, but the rabbi remained in the synagogue and sat down to study. The Baal Shem Tov sat down next to him and began singing a *niggun*—a melody. The rabbi did not want to be impolite to a guest to the town, so he did not interrupt and waited until the Besht finished his song. Then the rabbi greeted him. The Baal Shem Tov returned his greeting and sang another song. After he finished this one, the rabbi asked, "Why are you singing?"

"The people truly repented and their sins were forgiven!" How could I not sing?" replied the Besht.

"You're right!' said the rabbi.

"Let's dance!" said the Besht.

So the two of them jumped up, joined hands, and danced in joy.

Although this rabbi did not become a Hasid, a follower of the Baal Shem Tov, he was very impressed by the Besht and considered him a great person. He saw that the Besht was a Jew who sang and danced in joy when the sins of his fellow Jews were forgiven, and he was someone who could share that joy with him, the rabbi. While the Baal Shem Tov was in Slutzk, many rabbis and scholars were critical of him, but this rabbi rejected their disparaging comments.

The next day, the day of Yom Kippur Katan, two young Torah scholars were sitting in the synagogue studying. The Baal Shem Tov had noticed them the previous night. When the preacher had been speaking to arouse the congregation to repent, they had ignored his sermon and continued studying, sitting by themselves in the back of the synagogue. Such behavior was fairly typical of the scholars of that time, whose ideal in divine service was continuous, uninterrupted study; they felt free to separate from the congregation. So while everyone else was weeping in repentance, they sat and continued studying.

But this was not the Besht's attitude. He sat down next to these two young men and began to weep. When one of them asked him why he was weeping, he said,

"I'm weeping for you, because you're pushing God away by your arrogance. You're studying the Torah but forgetting the One who gave it."

"*Oy!* You're right!" said the young man, who was very moved by the Besht's words. How could you not be moved seeing someone weep for you? His study partner did remain distant, but this young scholar became a disciple of the Baal Shem Tov.[14] ◈

The Besht appreciated the theme of the preacher's sermon—that the ultimate purpose of Torah study and divine service is repentance. He saw that the preacher had touched people's hearts and brought them to repent. But the preacher did not fully understand the final part of the saying, that by repentance you attain the World to Come. He had led the congregation to tears of repentance; but if you truly repent and your sins are forgiven, you should be singing and dancing in joy. How much more should you be dancing if a whole congregation, a whole town, repents! That was what the Besht taught the rabbi. But the Besht's own joy came from an even deeper source, for the mystics teach that the World to Come is here now if one is immersed in the joy of God-consciousness.

When the Baal Shem Tov saw the two young scholars separate themselves from the congregation, ignoring Yom Kippur Katan and the preacher's sermon, it was clear to him that they did not understand that the true purpose of Torah study is to turn to God. How could you turn to God if you thought you did not need to repent and if you ignored the congregation when they were repenting?

The Besht was so devoted to God and to the Jewish people that after seeing the congregation repent, he sang and danced. But when he saw that two fine young men had become lost on the path of Torah, he wept for them. That is why he could turn people to God, for most people, when they see that someone loves them, love him in return and listen to his words with an open heart and mind.

The Baal Shem Tov felt an ecstatic closeness to his fellow Jews; he rejoiced at their good fortune and mourned at their misfortune. Just as he danced—in joyous ecstasy—that the townspeople had been forgiven, he wept—in an ecstasy of sorrow—at the misunderstanding and coldness of the two young scholars. Ecstasy is not only joyful. Ecstasy means that a person is in touch with his real self, with his deepest feelings, with his soul. A holy person like the Baal Shem Tov is always blissful, whether it is the bliss of sorrow or the bliss of joy.

The Joy of Jewishness

The Rabbis teach that the most primal joy to which a person has access rests not on any accomplishment but simply on being created by God in the divine image and by being alive in this wonderful and awesome world. But a Jew has a special joy. The Jewish people is heir to a great and ancient religious tradition that promises and delivers an ultimate spiritual fulfillment. Every morning, traditional Jews recite a blessing thanking God for being a son or daughter of this great tradition, for being created a Jew, and afterward sing a prayer with the words: "Happy are we, how goodly is our portion, how pleasant is our lot, and how beautiful is our heritage!" In a time of widespread assimilation, when many Jews have neglected their religious inheritance, it is good to be reminded that Jews who have always cherished their Judaism or have reclaimed their precious legacy possess a key to ecstasy in their joy at being Jewish.

Inheriting a Treasure

❦ As a young married man, Rabbi Levi Yitzhak of Berditchev lived with his father-in-law, who supported him, and studied Torah day and night; a Torah prodigy, he was destined to be a great rabbi and scholar.

Once, he returned from a trip he made to visit his rebbe and teacher, Rabbi Dov Ber, the Maggid of Mezritch, and was confronted by his father-in-law, who was upset that he "wasted his time" traveling to and from his rebbe instead of devoting every minute to Torah study (as was the non-Hasidic ideal). His father-in-law asked him why he needed to visit his teacher. What did he learn there that he could not learn from books? What was so important that he had to waste so much time on a long trip?

"I learned," answered Rabbi Levi Yitzhak, "that there is a Creator, who made the heavens and the earth!"

"Even the maid knows that!" scoffed his father-in-law, who called over the maid and asked her, "Is there a Creator?"

"Of course!" replied the maid.

"Do you see?" said the father-in-law triumphantly.

"She *says* it," replied Rabbi Levi Yitzhak with fire in his voice; "I *know* it." ◈

Rabbi Levi Yitzhak learned from his teacher, the Maggid of Mezritch, to know God from direct spiritual experience. Such personal knowledge of God leads to mystic joy. Rabbi Levi Yitzhak eventually became a great rebbe in Berditchev. He was famous for his religious ecstasy and, like some other rebbes, often danced ecstatically during prayers.

◈ Once, a Hasid saw him in the synagogue, dancing before the morning prayers had begun. After he had watched him for a while and the Berditchever finally stopped dancing, the Hasid asked him, "Rebbe, why are

you dancing before the prayers begin? I can understand
that you would dance during the prayers, but why now?"

Rebbe Levi Yitzhak answered, "When I just now
recited the morning blessing before the prayers, thanking God for creating me a Jew, I could not contain my
joy, for I inherited a great treasure that I in no way
worked for, so I had to begin dancing!"[1] ∾

What was the "great treasure" he inherited? As a Jew, he became heir to the Torah, to a tradition of God-knowledge that leads
to personal fulfillment and tremendous joy.

A Jew Lives Here!

∾ After the passing of Rabbi Dov Ber, the Maggid of
Mezritch, Rebbe Elimelech of Lizensk succeeded him as
leader of the Hasidic movement. When Rabbi Moshe
Leib of Sassov visited Rebbe Elimelech for the first time,
he was deeply moved by the rebbe's holiness and purity.

At the table during the Sabbath feast, Rebbe Elimelech honored Rabbi Moshe Leib by asking him to teach
some words of Torah. That week, the Torah portion read
in the synagogue tells how God smote the Egyptians
with the plague of the first born and passed over the
houses of the Israelites. Rabbi Moshe Leib said, "This
cannot possibly mean that God passed over a certain
place, because God is everywhere; there is no place
where He is not present. But the clue to understanding
what the verse means is to realize that the word translated 'to pass over' can also mean 'to leap' or 'to dance.'

What the verse means, then, is that when God came to the Egyptians' houses, He saw their idolatry and wickedness; but when He came to the Israelites' houses and saw their pure worship and their goodness, He was so overjoyed, He began, so to speak, to leap and dance and to cry out, 'A Jew lives here!'"

Rabbi Moshe Leib, ecstatically joyful at meeting the holy and pure Rebbe Elimelech, then jumped up on the table and began to dance, repeating over and over, "A Jew lives here! A Jew lives here!"[2] ◀◈▶

What does it mean to be a Jew? It means to love God, to love people, and to love the Torah. God Himself is so happy when a person is truly a Jew. And since our soul is a part of God, if we are in touch with our soul, we too will be happy when we see a real Jew, a person who is what a human should be.

A Real Jew

At the time the following story took place in Eastern Europe, most Jewish marriages were arranged. A boy would be married soon after his bar mitzvah, when he was fourteen, for example, and the girl thirteen. A scholarly boy usually went to live with his father-in-law, who supported him while he continued his Torah study until he became a Torah scholar or a rabbi. In this tale, the Rebbe of Sokolov tells a story in which he mentions his father-in-law, who was the town rabbi.

◀◈▶ The Hasidim of Rebbe Mendel of Sokolov once asked him who was the "most real Jew" he had ever met. The rebbe said, "When I was fourteen years old and married the daughter of the Rabbi of Sokolov, I moved from Kotzk—where I was living with my grandfather, the Kotzker Rebbe—to Sokolov, to live in the house of my father-in-law. I knew no one in town, and I was looking for one real Jew to befriend, because I learned from my holy grandfather, the Kotzker Rebbe, that God only loves what's real." [Dear reader, this simple sentence—that God only loves what's real—reflects the teaching of both the Kotzker Rebbe and Rabbi Shlomo Carlebach, from whom I heard the tale. It is worth the whole price of the story.]

The rebbe continued, "In every Jewish town, there are pious people who perform all of God's commandments, but I knew that it took something more than that to be a real Jew. I went into the synagogue and walked among the prestigious front rows and saw Torah scholars, rich people, and prominent people. But unfortunately, they were not real in that special way my grandfather had told me about. I then walked in the back rows, among the working people and the poor, and they were sweet, but unfortunately, they too were not real. I became sad, thinking to myself, 'How can I live in a town where I won't have one real Jew to befriend?'

"Suddenly, I lifted my head and my eye fell upon a simple, poor Jew standing behind the heating oven in the back of the synagogue reciting psalms. I saw God's glory on him. Was he praying! He knew how to stand before God, before the One and Only One. His light was shining. Was he real!

"I went up to him and asked, 'Who are you?'

"He replied, 'Moshe, Moshe the Water Carrier.'

"I tried very hard to become friends with Moshe, but he never responded. He was so humble, he could not imagine that I, the son-in-law of the rabbi, would want to be his friend. Whenever I went over to him in the synagogue and asked him, 'Moshe, how are you?' he would just answer, 'I'm fine,' and would continue to pray.

"One cold winter night, when I took a walk to get some fresh air, I reached the outskirts of the town and was walking back. I happened to pass by a broken house, and through an open window, I saw Moshe the Water Carrier standing in the middle of a circle of shoe-makers, tailors, and water carriers, holding an uplifted glass of wine in his hand as they danced around him. I swear to you, I saw God's glory shining on Moshe's face. I realized that this must be his house, and so I decided to walk in on his party.

"As I entered, Moshe met me at the door and said, 'Rabbi, what an honor.' [Although only fourteen, a boy with the family background of the Sokolover Rebbe was already ordained.]

"I said to him, 'Moshe, believe me, it's *my* honor to be in *your* home. Tell me, why are you celebrating?'

"It was obvious that none of those present knew the purpose of the celebration and so they all gathered around as he began to tell his story.

"He said, 'Rabbi, I grew up on the streets. My parents died when I was five years old. I knew very little about Judaism, only a little bit about how to pray and to recite psalms. No one ever took the time to teach me anything else. But you see, I'm a strong person, so I became a water carrier, because I could carry the heavy buckets on my shoulders. I married a woman who, believe me, when I married her, was the most beautiful woman in the world. But soon after our wedding, she was not beautiful anymore. She was filled with grief and pain because of the poverty in my house. As a water carrier, I make so little money. We have children, and when they were born, they were angels. But soon they were not angels anymore. They would cry all day for food: "Daddy, please give us something to eat—we're hungry! Buy us clothes to wear—we're cold!" The pain in my house was unbearable!

"'Rabbi, every night I wake up at three in the morning and my first delivery of the morning is to bring water to the synagogue for the people to wash their hands. I don't do this for money but to have the honor to bring water to cleanse the people before they pray. I am alone in the synagogue then, and so I open the holy Ark [containing the Torah scrolls].

"'I cry to the Almighty and say, "God in heaven, Master of the world, I am Moshe the Water Carrier from Sokolov. I am telling you, God in heaven, I can't live like this anymore. I can't bear the pain. I can't bear the hunger. Please, give me a hundred rubles so that I can start my life anew, so that I can live in dignity and feed my children!" You know, Rabbi, I have been doing this for years and years. I don't even know if I still believed that God would answer me.

"'But yesterday, the most unbelievable thing happened to me: When I was walking to the synagogue, bent over with the yoke of full water buckets on my shoulders, I was looking down, and although it was still dark, I saw by the light of the moon a pouch lying in the dust of the street. I opened it and found it contained one hundred rubles. I said to myself, Are these the one hundred rubles that I've been praying for all these years? They must be!

"'So I went into the synagogue, opened the holy Ark, and said, "God, Master of the universe, thank You, thank You *so much* for listening to my prayers. It's true, You are the Master of the world, and You hear the prayers of every human being." I added, "God, let this be a secret between me and You just for today."

"'I was ecstatic. Rabbi, you know how heavy the full water buckets are? Well, they were not heavy yesterday. I danced with them from house to house. Suddenly, I was in paradise. I came home later, and I swear to you, my wife looked as beautiful as on our wedding day and my children were angels again. Everything was beautiful, and all day long I blessed people, I blessed God.

"'At night, I returned to the synagogue for the afternoon and evening prayers and saw a great commotion there. Do you remember, Rabbi, two weeks ago, Avraham died and left a wife, Hanna, with eleven children? The whole community had collected a hundred rubles for Hanna. She was standing by the door, weeping and saying that somehow she had lost the hundred rubles! I went back behind the oven to pray, but I automatically closed my prayer book. I said, "God in heaven, this is the last time You will see me in the synagogue. If You want to give me a hundred rubles, do You have to give me Hanna's hundred rubles? God, You are cruel. I don't want to know You anymore. I don't want to be Your servant anymore. You'll never see me in the synagogue again!" I put down my prayer book and ran home.

"'As I ran, everything looked black. I was suffering. I was as if in hell. I was lost and didn't know what to do.

"'When I got home, I felt miserable. My wife looked ugly again and my children looked terrible. I hated the whole world. I did not want to know anyone anymore. I went to sleep. But how could I sleep? I put the pillow over my face. I did not want my wife to see how much I was crying. I tossed and turned on my bed for hours. Late at night, suddenly, I heard my own soul crying, "Moshe the Water Carrier, what happened to you? All your life you trusted in God, you believed in God, and now when you need Him the most, why don't you turn to Him? Why don't you pray to the One, to the Only One, who hears every prayer?"

"'Rabbi, I poured out my heart to God like never before and said, "God, I'm lost, I'm miserable, I don't know what to do. I am begging You, please, let me hear Your voice. Tell me what to do." And Rabbi, *I swear to you, I heard God's voice,* and God said to me, "Moshe the Water Carrier, get up fast and take the money to Hanna, the wife of Avraham. The money is not yours. It's hers!"

"'Suddenly, I was back in paradise. Everything was good and beautiful again. I got dressed fast. I ran to

Hanna's house and even though it was totally dark, in the middle of the night, I felt surrounded by a heavenly light. When I arrived at Hanna's house, I knocked on the door. She opened the door and still had sleep in her eyes. She said, "Moshe, what are you doing here at this hour? What do you want?"

"'I said, "Hanna, I found your money. Here it is!" I tell you, Rabbi, if you only could have seen her eyes when she said, "Thank you, Moshe." Even if God gave me all the rubles in the world, it wouldn't compare to what I felt at that moment. I knew that perhaps my life would never change, that my children would never have proper clothes or have enough to eat. But I knew what it felt like to be a Jew!

"'So tonight I am celebrating, thanking God for answering my prayers, thanking God for giving me the strength to act like a Jew and return the money.'"

The Sokolover Rebbe ended his story, saying, "I joined Moshe, the holy water carrier, and his friends— the shoemakers, tailors, and water carriers—and we danced for hours. Moshe danced because God had given him the strength to return the money and do what was right. I danced because I had found a real Jew."[3]

The Bach's Partner
in Heaven

Rabbi Yoel Sirkes was one of the greatest Torah scholars in Jewish history. He was called the Bach, after the acronym of the title of his most famous book, the *Bayit Chadash* (New House).

⫘ The Bach wanted to know who would be his next-door neighbor in the Garden of Eden, because the Jewish tradition teaches that everyone has a neighbor or partner in paradise, someone whose spiritual qualities and virtues are somehow equivalent to his own. The Bach was curious, so he asked in heaven and they told him, "There is a rich Jew named Yankeleh in Lemberg; he will be your neighbor."

The Bach went to Lemberg, imagining that Yankeleh, his partner in paradise, probably studies Torah day and night and that he prays with unbelievable devotion and fervor. The Bach himself was so devoted to God, Torah, and the Jewish people; certainly his neighbor in paradise must be somebody special!

The Bach arrived in Lemberg, went to this rich Jew's home and asked for hospitality. Yankeleh was very happy to receive him. After all, the Bach was one of the greatest rabbis! The Bach carefully watched Yankeleh, to see what kind of person he was. He turned out to be a fine Jew: he prayed regularly; he gave charity generously according to his wealth. But he was *nothing special!* The Bach was there for one week, and he was actually disgusted. He thought to himself, "I'm giving my life for God and the Jewish people day and night, and this is all I'll have, this simple Jew as my neighbor?" He was just about to leave when he heard that Yankeleh was marrying off his son the following week. So he decided to stay for the wedding.

At the ceremony, the Bach watched as his host, Yankeleh, walked with his son to the bridal canopy.

Then, suddenly, Yankeleh heard someone sobbing from
the depths of his heart. This was a celebration--every-
one in town was invited, including all the poor people;
why was someone crying? Yankeleh stopped and he said
to one of his servants, "Please go see who's crying
there." The servant came back and told him, "There's a
boy, the same age as the bridegroom"—who was about
fifteen years old—"who's crying."

Yankeleh said, "Bring him here."

They brought him over. The boy was in rags.
Yankeleh said to him, "Why are you crying?"

The boy said, "Do you really want to know?"

He said, "Tell me."

"Do you remember," said the boy, "that rich Jew
who went bankrupt last year? I'm his son. I was engaged to the bride, the girl that your son is going to
marry. I've been engaged to her my whole life. [In those
days of arranged marriages, some people engaged their
children when they were three or four years old.] We
love each other so much. But because my father went
bankrupt, her parents did not want her to marry me,
a penniless boy. So they broke the engagement and engaged her to marry your son, because you're rich."

Yankeleh said to his servant, "Please, call the bride."
They brought the girl over and he asked her, "Is it true
that you were engaged to this boy all those years?"

She said, "Yes."

"Is it true that you love him the most?"

"Yes," she said, "it's true, I love him the most, but
my parents won't let me marry him!"

"Oh," said Yankeleh. "Thank you *so much* for telling me! Thank you *so much!*"

He turned to his son and said, "Did you hear this? I'll find you a girl who will be your true soulmate. But now, go back to the house. Take this boy with you and exchange clothes with him. Put on what he's wearing, and give him your new suit."

And he said to the boy, "I want you to know that I am going to treat you as if you were my own son. All the money and gifts I was going to give to my son, I'm giving to you."

When the Bach told this story, he would say, "I've never seen a father dance at the wedding of his *own* son with as much joy as this man danced at the wedding of this boy he didn't know, whom he reunited with his intended bride.

"When I came to Lemberg, I couldn't understand why he deserved to sit next to me in paradise; when I left, I couldn't understand how I deserved to sit next to him."[4] ❧

That everyone has a partner or neighbor in paradise goes back to the Talmud, which tells of a great Torah scholar whose partner in paradise was a simple man, great not in Torah knowledge but in his good deeds. Yankeleh was a fine but ordinary Jew when it came to the conventional measures of religiosity—his praying, his charity, and so on—but his open-hearted generosity and kindness made him equal to one of the greatest rabbis of his time.

It was Yankeleh's selfless compassion that led to his ecstatic dancing. Undoubtedly, his soul was very happy when he gave so much to the poor boy he had never before met and acted like a real Jew.

Even the Least Devotion Is Precious

Rebbe Nachman of Bratzlav taught that a Jew should always be joyful because even the least devotion to God is precious. He often recommended finding one's good points and rejoicing over them. He
said, "Sadness is a despicable trait. One must keep oneself from it
completely. One must encourage and uplift oneself. A person must
realize that every time he makes even the slightest movement to
serve God, it is precious in God's eyes. This is true even if that person moves himself by a single hairsbreadth. Since a person exists
in the lower World of Action,⁵ every spiritual or physical movement
and change of place is extremely difficult and therefore precious in
God's eyes." To illustrate this teaching, Rebbe Nachman created
and told the following fictional story.

≈ There was once a tzaddik who became very depressed and melancholy. When depression and melancholy afflicted him, they were a great burden to him
that was hard to bear. Matters became worse and worse
until he was so depressed and overcome by heaviness
that he could not move even the least bit from his place;
he became almost completely immobile.

He wanted to make himself joyful and uplift himself, but it was impossible for him to do anything. Whenever he found some good trait in himself or some good
deed that he had done, which would cheer him, the Evil
One found in it something improper that would sadden
him. Therefore, it was impossible for him to do anything
to make himself happy, since in everything joyful that
could uplift him, he also found something sad that depressed him.

Finally, the tzaddik began to meditate on the morning blessing thanking God for the joy of being created a Jew. This could undoubtedly be a source of unlimited joy. Because even the lowest Jew, despite his faults, is still so holy! When he reflected on God's kindness in making him a Jew, he could certainly be happy. And this is a source of joy that has in it no sadness. When a person tries to find joy in something he himself did, it is possible to find sadness in every joy. No matter what he did, he can always find shortcomings, and he will not be able to uplift himself and be happy. But there is no sadness at all in God's having made him a Jew. That is from God Himself, who had pity on him and created him a Jew; how could he find anything wrong in that, since it is from God? Because certainly, regardless of his own many faults, he is still a Jew because God made him a Jew! And merely being a Jew is so precious! The tzaddik began to make himself joyful about this. He rejoiced and uplifted himself little by little, each time more and more until he was full of great joy, until he reached the level of joy experienced by Moses when he went up to receive the Tablets.

Through this uplifting he was able to fly many thousands of miles into the supernal worlds. He then saw himself, and he was very far from the place where he had been originally, which bothered him very much. He felt that when he descended, he would be very far away from his original place. When it was discovered that he had disappeared, people would consider it a great miracle. The tzaddik did not want such publicity, since he always wanted to walk modestly with God."

Finally, the joy began to decrease; joy has a limit, and it begins and ends by itself. When it began to lessen, it did so little by little. The tzaddik therefore descended little by little, coming down from the place to which he had flown during his time of joy. He eventually returned to the place from which he had ascended. He was very surprised, since he was in exactly the same place where he had been at first. Looking at himself, he realized that he had not moved at all, or if he had moved, it had been at most by a hairsbreadth. He had moved so little that no one other than God could measure it. The tzaddik was very surprised at this. He had flown so far, through so many worlds, and at the same time here below he had not moved at all.

This showed him how precious even the slightest movement is in God's eyes. When a person moves himself even a hairsbreadth in this world, it can be considered as more than thousands of miles and even thousands of worlds.

This can be understood, said Rebbe Nachman, when we realize that the physical world is no more than the central point in the midst of the astronomical spheres. This is known to the masters of astronomy. And compared to the supernal spiritual worlds, the entire physical universe is no more than a dot. When lines extend from a central point, the closer they are to the point, the closer they are to one another. The farther they extend from the point, the farther the lines get from one another. Therefore, when the lines are very far from the point, they are also very far apart. This is true even though near the central point, they are extremely close to one another.

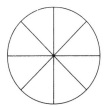

If one imagined lines drawn from the earth to the upper astronomical spheres, one would see that even if one moved a hairsbreadth down below, the movement would be reflected as a motion of thousands of miles in the upper spheres. It would be in the same ratio as the spheres are higher than the earth. The spheres must be very huge, since there are stars without number, and each star is at least as large as our planet.[7]

This is all the more certainly true when one considers the supernal worlds, compared to which even the highest astronomical spheres are like nothing. Therefore, the distance between these extending lines in the upper worlds is without measure. A movement of less than a hairsbreadth, so small that only God can measure it, can consist of a passage through thousands of worlds and thousands of miles in the supernal worlds. How much more is this true when one travels a mile or more to serve God. When a person serves God the least bit, it is

so precious that the reward cannot even be imagined;
as the prophet Isaiah said, "No eye has seen it."⁸

    This section began with a story of the ecstatic dancing of
Rebbe Levi Yitzhak of Berditchev, when he recited the morning
blessing about being created a Jew. It ends with Rebbe Nachman of
Bratzlav explaining that joy.

The Joy of Sabbaths and Holidays

Sabbaths and holidays are special times for holy happiness. The peaceful Sabbaths are times for delight and bliss (*oneg* and *menuha*); the holidays, which infuse dynamic spiritual energies into religious life, are times for joy and gladness (*simha* and *sasson*). We discussed in the Introduction the ancient rabbinic teaching that a mourner is not permitted to enter a celebration in the king's palace. Rebbe Shalom Noah Berzhovsky, the late Slonimer Rebbe in Jerusalem, applied this thought to Sabbaths and holidays. He wrote:

> Joy, singing, and dancing are of the essence of the divine service of Sabbaths and holidays. The Rabbis said, "A person not joyful on the holy Sabbath is like someone who goes to the palace on a day when the king is celebrating, and is sad. They will not allow him to participate in the celebration, even if he is one of the king's ministers. But someone wholeheartedly joyful, even if he is only a simple villager, will be asked to take part. Thus by a Jew's inner joy on Sabbaths and holidays, he merits being invited into the innermost chambers of the King's palace."[1]

Jewish religious law forbids many kinds of labor on the Sabbath in order to provide one full day of peace and rest each week to engage in spiritual pursuits. Only those who keep the Sabbath and refrain from work can taste its peaceful delight, as the Sabbath prayer says: "The people who hallow the seventh day shall all be sated and delighted with God's goodness." Rabbi Noson Tzvi Finkel, the Elder of Slobodka—a great leader of the pietist Musar movement, which focuses on ethics and perfection of character—taught that the essence of all the Torah's commandments is to produce delight, and that is especially so for the Sabbath, about which the Torah says, "You shall call the Sabbath a delight."[2]

Festive meals are a part of Sabbath joy. Traditional Jews pray three times on the Sabbath—Friday night, Saturday morning, and late Saturday afternoon—and in honor of the day, they eat three meals, one after each prayer service. Another way the Sabbath becomes a delight is by the custom of Sabbath hospitality, of entertaining friends and strangers at meals, rejoicing and causing others to rejoice.

While all three yearly "pilgrimage"[3] festivals—*Sukkot* (the Festival of Booths), *Pesach* (Passover), and *Shavuot* (the Festival of Weeks)—are joyous, Sukkot, commemorating the Jews' sojourn in the Sinai Desert after the Exodus, when they dwelt in booths—is especially joyous and is referred to as "the season of our rejoicing." During the eight days of Sukkot, traditional Jews fulfill the *mitzvot* (commandments) to build a *sukkah* (booth) and to spend as much time in it as possible—eating, studying Torah, relaxing, even sleeping there. When a person knows that his sojourn in this world is like a stay in a temporary booth and he trusts in the eternal God, he experiences a season of rejoicing.

The holiday of Simhat Torah (Joy of the Torah), which follows Sukkot, has joy in its very name. Simhat Torah brings the joy of Sukkot to a culmination. On this day, to celebrate God's precious gift of the Torah to the Jewish people, Jews remove all the Torah scrolls from the Ark and sing and dance with them around the synagogue.

The final holiday mentioned in this section is *Tu BeShvat,* known as the "New Year of the Trees" (the name itself is its date on the Hebrew calendar). It is a mystic celebration anticipating the return to the bliss of the Garden of Eden; it is the only holiday ordained by the kabbalists. On Tu BeShvat, kabbalists and others celebrate the renewed flow of divine life-energy from the cosmic Tree of Life into the world by ritually eating fruit with spiritual intentions.[4]

Sabbaths and holidays begin and end in the evening. Both Sabbaths and most holidays are inaugurated in the evening, when the woman of the house lights candles in the home, and honored later, after the evening synagogue service, when the man of the house recites the *kiddush,* the blessing of sanctification over a cup of wine before the meal. The candles symbolize the extra divine light added by the holy day; the wine symbolizes the intoxicating divine bliss and joy of God's presence.

The Parable of the King's Letter

The Baal Shem Tov taught that whereas the weekdays' spirituality is more focused on the body, *Shabbat* (the Sabbath) is the day of the soul. He said, "The essence of Shabbat is to cleave to God, blessed be He, in *d'vekut* through Torah study, prayer, and meditation in purity. That is why the holy *Zohar* says about Shabbat: 'This day is the day of the soul, not the day of the body'—meaning that the Root of All Souls shines into the souls that are in bodies, and they yearn for Him; that is the extra soul power available on Shabbat. Those who are pure of heart actually feel this."[5]

The Besht taught that the true mystic joy of the Sabbath is the joy of the soul but that the body also has to be brought in to the joy, in its own way. To explain why, he told a parable about the reason for Sabbath feasts.

⇛ A king's son was sent by his father on a mission to a small village in a distant country, where he lived among common and coarse people. After a long time had passed, a letter from his father, the king, reached him, and he was so elated that he wanted to celebrate. He was worried, though, that the villagers would ridicule him, saying, "Why is today special? He's making a fool of himself!" So he made a party for all the villagers and gave them wine and liquor in abundance. Then, while they were rejoicing in their drunkenness, he could rejoice in his happiness over his father's love, without being noticed.

"That is the reason," said the Besht, "that we entertain and divert the body by eating three meals on the Sabbath. For the soul, which is like a king's son, is ashamed to rejoice in front of the body, which is like a villager. So while the body rejoices in its things, the soul can rejoice in its *d'vekut* with its Father, the King, the Holy One, blessed be He."⁶ ⊰⊱

On Shabbat, one enjoys the pleasures of life on different levels, both sensual and spiritual. And when the body rejoices in food and drink, or in other physical pleasures, extra power is added to the soul, which rejoices in things of the soul.

The Two Thrones

⊰⊱ When the Baal Shem Tov was a young man and still seeking the correct way to serve God, he was often anxious and worried that he was not performing God's commandments in the proper way. He was so fearful of sin that he made himself depressed, as he was constantly troubled that he was not serving God to the fullest extent, as He should be served. The Baal Shem Tov was particularly concerned about his Sabbath observance, because the many rules restricting Sabbath activity are very complicated and detailed, and it is difficult to follow them all perfectly. Indeed, there are countless intricate legal requirements in the Torah; who can adhere to all of them without some fault or deficiency?

Now, according to Jewish tradition, the prophet Elijah appears to mystic adepts in visions to teach them Torah secrets. The Baal Shem Tov, being a special soul, merited being taught by the biblical prophet Ahiyah, from the town of Shiloh, who was Elijah's own teacher and master. So one Sabbath, the Baal Shem Tov asked his heavenly teacher and master, the prophet Ahiyah the Shilonite, to show him the place in the Garden of Eden reserved for those who most perfectly observe the Sabbath. Ahiyah took the Besht on a soul ascent (in which the soul exits the body and ascends to heaven), leading him higher and higher, from one chamber to another in the heavenly palace, until they ascended to a place so high and exalted that even the angels and seraphim (fiery angels) are not permitted to enter. He saw what no eye had ever been privileged to see. In this exalted chamber, a table was set for a heavenly banquet, and at its head were two radiant golden thrones inlaid with sparkling diamonds and precious jewels.

The Baal Shem Tov asked his master, Ahiyah, "For whom are these two glorious thrones prepared?"

"One throne is for you," said Ahiyah, "if you are wise, and the other is for a companion whom you must find." What he meant was that the Baal Shem Tov would

merit the second of the two thrones if he followed the
perfect Sabbath ways of this other person, for whom
the first throne was reserved; the Besht would become
this person's partner in the Garden of Eden.

That night, at the conclusion of the Sabbath, after
the Saturday night *havdalah* ceremony, which sepa-
rates the holy Sabbath from the profane weekdays that
follow, the Baal Shem Tov ordered his servant Alexei to
prepare his horses and coach at once, and he set out
to find this person who kept the Sabbath the best and
might be his companion in paradise. After they left
the vicinity of the town, they traveled with miraculous
speed, covering vast distances in a short time. The
Besht, being a kabbalist who knew the divine Names
that activated different supernal powers, used the divine Name for shortening a journey, by which the earth
contracted under the racing hooves of his horses. He
had Alexei drop the reins and turn around to sit facing
backward, in the opposite direction, while the horses
sped forward on their own, under divine guidance, to
the place the Besht needed to go.

They traveled enormous distances. The destination
was far away, and although they traveled speedily, the
trip still took days. The horses raced on and on; they
crossed mountains and valleys, fields and forests,
rivers and lakes, until the Baal Shem Tov arrived in a
large foreign city where no Jews resided. Finally, the
horses stopped in front of a house on the outskirts of
the city, indicating that this was the place the Besht
was seeking.

The Besht knocked on the door, and a man, who was Jewish but did not have a beard, wear a yarmulke, or otherwise dress as a Jew, came out and greeted him. The Besht spoke to him in a foreign language and asked if he could receive hospitality for a few days. The man said yes and warmly welcomed his guest into his home. After a short while, however, the Besht noted, to his surprise, that the man did not in any way follow a Jewish lifestyle or practice Jewish customs. There seemed to be nothing Jewish about him! Was this the person who kept the Sabbath perfectly? He did not dress Jewishly, he ate nonkosher food and did not wash his hands before eating; neither did he make blessings over food or pray! Was this to be his companion in paradise?

But the Besht reasoned that if this was the place where his horses had stopped, this must be the man he had to find. His strange host *must* be holy and special; it was simply that his holiness was concealed! The Besht therefore decided that he should wait and observe the man carefully. Nevertheless, after even the most thorough scrutiny, he realized to his dismay that there was nothing remotely Jewish about him, let alone holy!

The Besht spent the Sabbath there as well. After all, he had been told that this was the man who kept the Sabbath most perfectly! Needless to say, the Besht's own Sabbath was dismal, for there was no kosher food in the house, certainly no traditional Sabbath foods, such as fish or hot *cholent* stew. All he was able to eat were a few loaves of dry bread that he had taken along for the trip. Neither could he read the Torah portion, as is customary on the Sabbath, for there was no Torah scroll available.

Although the Besht closely watched everything the man did, he detected no shred of Sabbath observance. This from the man who "kept the Sabbath best"! On Saturday afternoon, the man hosted a large party to which he invited his many gentile friends. Men and women mixed freely as they ate, drank, and danced together; the men smoked cigars on the Sabbath—all forbidden by Jewish law and custom! The Besht's host was in a happy mood at this party and was rushing about, doing everything possible to entertain his friends and put them in good spirits. But what a disappointing Sabbath for the Baal Shem Tov, who, of course, did not participate in this raucous merriment! He became deeply depressed, thinking to himself, "Will this coarse, unspiritual person, who is committing all these sins desecrating the Sabbath, be my partner in the Garden of Eden?"

Discouraged and confused, the Besht was about to leave on Saturday night after making *havdalah.* But before departing, he asked his host, out of curiosity, "What were you celebrating earlier in the day?"

The man answered, "I'll tell you the truth: I'm a Jew, but I know nothing about Judaism. I was orphaned when I was just a little boy and was adopted by gentiles and taken far from where I was born. But one thing I remember about my parents: on Saturday afternoon, they would make a great feast for all their neighbors and do everything possible to make them happy. So I try to be a good Jew in the only way I know, by rejoicing on the

Sabbath and making a party for my neighbors. That is my Judaism, and I do it with all my heart and soul!"

The Besht then realized that this man was actually pious and holy and had a true Jewish heart. He had an exalted soul, for how many people taken from their Jewish homes and raised in similar circumstances would act as he did, to do the one thing he knew about Judaism with such faith and devotion?

The Besht wanted to return this great soul to its Jewish root and explain to him in detail all the laws of Sabbath observance and tell him how Jews really keep the Sabbath. But when the Baal Shem Tov tried to open his mouth to speak, he felt something pressing down on his tongue. The great tzaddikim have trained all their limbs to do only the will of God: their eyes do not see what they should not see, their ears do not hear what they should not hear, and their tongue does not speak what should not be said. On reflection, the Besht realized that heaven had removed his power of speech to prevent him from explaining the Sabbath to the man, for if he would know all the myriad Sabbath laws, how would he, with his meager background, ever be able to keep all of them? As he was, he was a holy person, but if he would learn all the rules and regulations, he would never attain even an average observance. God was more pleased with the unusual way he kept the Sabbath now than if he changed his ways and abided by all the Sabbath laws. Now, his Sabbath was with all his heart, with pious simplicity and joy. So he was a very high soul. If he were to know the traditionally correct way to keep the Sabbath, he would never reach that exalted level. His observance would fall short, and inevitably, the happiness that he felt in the Sabbath, which he kept faithfully according to his own capabilities and capacity of understanding, would disappear. This experience taught the Baal Shem Tov a great lesson not only about the Sabbath but also about all other religious practices: that the main thing is not how much you do but that everything you do is done with delight and joy.

The Baal Shem Tov then returned home and asked his master, Ahiyah the Shilonite, to show him the place in the next world reserved for those who keep the Sabbath most poorly. Ahiyah led him through barren deserts and past the Mountains of Darkness into a cave. They descended more and more deeply until they finally reached hell, and then they continued farther and farther down, through dark and dismal chambers, until they reached the lowest pit in hell. There the Besht saw two coal-black thrones, smoldering and smoking and emanating an acrid odor.

"For whom are these terrible thrones prepared?" asked the Besht of his master, Ahiyah.

"One throne will be for you," replied Ahiyah, "if you are unwise, and the second one will be for a companion whom you must find."

The Besht understood that if he kept the Sabbath according to the misguided ways of this possible companion, he would inherit the second of those two thrones of punishment.

On Friday afternoon, the Baal Shem Tov set out to find this person who kept the Sabbath most poorly. He told his coach driver to let the horses go their own way. This time the trip was short and brief. Soon they were in a nearby town, traveling through a densely populated Jewish neighborhood that was bustling with activity in preparation for the Sabbath. Because the Sabbath begins at dusk on Friday night and no purchases can be made once the Sabbath has begun, everything has to be taken care of in advance. As the Besht's coach raced through the narrow streets, they saw Jews hurrying to and from the market making their final purchases for the holy day of rest. The Besht could smell the delectable odors of Sabbath cooking coming from the Jewish homes as he passed by in his coach. Finally, the horses came to a stop in front of a house from which could be heard the chanting of Torah study. When the Besht climbed down from the coach, he discovered that it was the house of the town rabbi, who strictly adhered to the minutest details of religious observance.

The Besht knocked on the door and was let in by a servant, but he had to wait; he could not speak to the rabbi, who was too engrossed in Torah study to look up and greet a guest. It is a holy thing to lose oneself in Torah study, but when a guest comes, one should notice. The Sages teach that Abraham left off speaking with God Himself to greet his three visitors, who were angels that appeared in human disguise. The Besht waited patiently for half an hour until the rabbi finished his study session and, looking up and noticing him, offered him a weak greeting. "May I stay with you for the Sabbath?" asked the Besht. The rabbi consented, ordered his servant to care for the Besht's accommodations, and went back to his studying. Hardly a warm welcome!

That Sabbath was a miserable one for the Besht. Gloom and darkness pervaded the rabbi's house. The rabbi was so afraid of violating the prohibition against touching any work implement, such as a pen, which one is forbidden to use on the Sabbath, that he would not stretch out his hand. It is holy to have such great fear of sin, but he carried it to extremes! He was so afraid of stepping on an ant—for one is forbidden to kill any living creature, even a noxious insect, on the holy Sabbath—that he would not stretch out his foot. This too is undoubtedly holy—isn't such reverence for life beautiful?—but he took it to extremes! As a result, he could not stretch out his hand or his foot and he sat, with hands and feet tucked in, like a prisoner, in his chair throughout the Sabbath day.

The Besht understood that this rabbi's Sabbath observance aroused displeasure in heaven, and he wanted to explain to the rabbi how to truly keep the Sabbath with joy and delight. But when the Besht opened his mouth to speak, no words came out, and he felt something pressing down on his tongue. On reflection, he realized that heaven did not want him to instruct the rabbi. The Sages teach that it is a *mitzvah*, a divine commandment, to instruct someone who will listen to you; but if you know that he will *not* listen, it is a *mitzvah* to refrain from instructing him, for you will only cause unnecessary argument and strife. This rabbi was so proud of his Torah scholarship and so sure of his own way that he would never accept instruction from the Baal Shem Tov.

From these two visits and experiences, the Baal Shem Tov learned the importance of keeping the Sabbath and all of the Torah's commandments joyfully. Previously, he had been constantly anxious that he was not serving God properly, but now he had learned that an excessive fear of sin, which produces guilt, anxiety, and gloom, gives God no pleasure. From that time on, the Besht realized that a Jew must delight in the Sabbath and in doing God's will and must not allow fear of sin and transgression to stifle the joy he derives from Judaism.[7] ☜

According to the Baal Shem Tov and other Hasidic rebbes, a person who observes every detail of the Sabbath rules, without experiencing the Sabbath's delight and bliss, has missed out on the essence. But someone who enjoys the Sabbath's peace and bliss, even while failing to observe all its rules perfectly, has truly kept the Sabbath's essence.

Rebbe Yaakov Yitzhak of Pshis'cha, who was called "the Holy Jew," said that the only way a person could perfectly observe all the minute regulations of the Sabbath was if he was bound hand and foot for the whole day. But then, he said, he would not be able to fulfill the central obligation of the day, to experience *oneg* Shabbat, Sabbath bliss! The man "bound hand and foot" is like the rabbi of the Baal Shem Tov tale, who sat with his hands and feet tucked in because of his fear of sin. The point of the Holy Jew's teaching and of the story too is that a person should not make himself miserable worrying about the details of religious observance, lest he miss the

essence of the Sabbath and of Judaism—the bliss and joy of God's
nearness.

Sabbath like the Chernovitzer

Rebbe Hayim of Chernovitz was passionately in love with the Sabbath. His Sabbath ecstasy was famous.

❧ There was a wealthy Hungarian cattle dealer who
once took fifteen hundred thalers and traveled to Romania to buy livestock in the cattle market. While there, he
happened to see on the street a remarkable man—whose
face radiated holiness—walking around collecting donations. He asked passersby who the person was and
was told that it was Rebbe Hayim of Chernovitz, who
was collecting money to ransom people imprisoned for
debts. In Jewish tradition, ransoming captives is considered a most sacred deed. When the merchant asked
them about Rebbe Hayim, they told him that he was a
holy man—which was obvious from his appearance—and
that he was extraordinarily devoted to the Sabbath; on
the Sabbath, he was actually a head taller than on
weekdays!

The cattle dealer, who was so taken with the evident spiritual nobility of the rebbe, went over to the
rebbe, introduced himself, and asked him how much
money he needed to collect. The rebbe said fifteen
hundred thalers. When asked how much he had already
collected, he said, "Twelve thalers." But he was not discouraged. He would just persevere until he had the full

amount. The cattle dealer was unhappy at the thought of the rebbe's having to go around collecting one coin here, another there, and said to him, "Rebbe, I'll give you the full fifteen hundred." The rebbe took the money—which was everything the merchant had—and gave him the twelve thalers he had already collected so that the merchant would have enough money to get home.

Rebbe Hayim then asked him what blessing he would like in return for his goodness and charity. The merchant said that he wanted to experience the Sabbath as the rebbe experienced it. "That's something else," said Rebbe Hayim. "I'm not sure about that."

The man said, "Rebbe, when I gave you the money, I didn't bargain with you. I gave you the whole amount without questions." So the rebbe said, "I'll bless you for that on one condition: that from Thursday night on, you cease work and begin preparing for the Sabbath."

The Sabbath begins Friday night, so the rebbe was asking him to devote Thursday night and Friday during the day to preparing spiritually for the Sabbath. The man agreed, and the rebbe blessed him.

When the merchant went home to his town in Hungary, his wife asked him where the cattle he bought were. He told her, "I bought some better merchandise." From then on, he adhered faithfully to Rebbe Hayim's condition. He completed all his business by Thursday afternoon. His workweek was Monday to Thursday afternoon. (On Sunday, after the Sabbath, he was in no condition to work.)

On Sabbath eve, powerful feelings of holiness already began to surge within him. His mood deepened perceptibly at dusk, when his wife lit the candles to usher in the Sabbath. When he prayed the Sabbath-welcoming service, he began to ascend. When he sang the opening words of the first prayer, "Let us sing to the Lord!"—he flew into another world. When he recited the "Hear O Israel!" prayer, *Sh'ma Yisrael*—he flew still higher. He had to be helped home after the service, being intoxicated with the holy joy of the Sabbath and unsteady on his feet, as if actually drunk.

After a number of years of this kind of Sabbath, he reached the spiritual level where he became a rebbe and taught many Hasidim. [8] ◈

How can a person make himself a fit vessel for the Sabbath's powerful light, for its joy and bliss? By preparing for it beforehand—as in the Chernovitzer's condition for the merchant. Yet even that is not enough to achieve Sabbath ecstasy like that of the Chernovitzer. The merchant had opened his heart in an act of selfless charity but still needed to win the rebbe's blessing, which transmitted his Sabbath ecstasy. The merchant had given charity without limits, and as a reward, he received Sabbath ecstasy without limits. This tale gives us a precious glimpse into the bliss and delight of those who truly taste the Sabbath's divine sweetness.

Hasidic Snowmen

◈ Rabbi Moshe of Lelov was the son of Rebbe David of Lelov, and his friend, Rabbi Yitzhak of Vorki, was a top disciple of Rabbi Moshe's father. Later in life, both young men became rebbes.

One Sabbath night during the winter, when it was snowing, the two friends, Rabbi Moshe and Rabbi Yitzhak, went out together to an isolated spot to dance in honor of the holy Sabbath and to rejoice in the kingdom of God. Both of them always worked to hide their fiery piety from others, but here, away from prying eyes, they burst out in stormy song and danced ecstatically, without tiring, the whole night. They were elevated handbreadths above the earth and rose into the upper world. Sparks of fire flew from their dancing feet, and their strong voices echoed to a great distance.

The whole forest danced with them. The trees swayed, and the birds joined them in singing, like what is written in the mystic Book of Song that tells which song each species sings in praise of the Creator. The whole universe was dancing with them, as in the words of the Sabbath hymn that they sang: "Let those who keep the Sabbath rejoice in Your kingdom!" Yes, yes, rejoice in Your kingdom alone! Not in this world, not in the World to Come, but in Your kingdom alone!

Large slabs of snow dropped heavily from the tree branches while feathery snowflakes fell from the sky the whole night and landed on the two young tzaddikim who danced, lost in ecstasy, in a circle and did not even feel the snow piling up on their heads and bodies. They saw and heard nothing; they were burning up with the fire of the holy Sabbath!

Dawn came, and from a distance, some passersby were amazed to see two large mounds of snow trundling this way and that between the trees, circling in dance.

That is how the two young tzaddikim were "caught," so to speak, and the mask with which they concealed themselves—in order to serve God modestly—was lifted ever so slightly.[9] ◄◊►

By ceasing to work and resting on the Sabbath, Jews give witness that God created the heavens and the earth and all that is in them. These two holy youths cherished the Sabbath, rejoiced in God's kingdom, and joined with all creation in praising the Creator, as it says in the verse of the Sabbath hymn they sang: "Let those who keep the Sabbath and call it a delight, a holy joy, rejoice in Your kingdom!"

A Hasid Persecuted for His Joy

◄◊► One Sukkot, a venerable Karliner Hasid, a renowned storyteller named Rabbi Aharon Asher, and some fellow Hasidim were sitting in his *sukkah* engaged in an animated discussion about joy. Of all the Jewish holidays, Sukkot is especially joyful, being called in the tradition "the season of our rejoicing." After filling his glass with liquor and toasting his comrades with "*L'hayim!*"— "To life!"—Rabbi Aharon Asher spoke.

"Let me tell you a tale that relates to Sukkot and also to the subject we are discussing—joy. A person certainly should rejoice, and Rebbe Aharon of Karlin says that even the least joy, of even the lowest sort, comes from a holy source. The main thing is not to be trapped, God forbid, by sadness and depression, because sadness is actually hell itself, may God save us! Listen to this tale, which teaches that lesson.

"In a certain town there lived a Jew whom everybody called Reb Abish the Hasid because he was truly pious as a Hasid should be. Although he was terribly poor, he never complained about his situation and was never overbearing with another person. He was satisfied with what he had, which was very little. He cast his burden on the Lord, trusted in Him, and received everything—suffering included—that came his way with love of God. To everything that happened, he uttered the traditional pious saying: 'Everything that God does is for good.' His face radiated joy, not only on Sabbaths and holidays but on all the days of the year. At all times, there was joy in his house. He was happy, cheerful, and exhilarated with the joy of being alive.

"In that same town there lived another Jew, Reb Getzel the Rich Man. People gossiped that he had been influenced by atheistic views and, from thinking too much about matters hidden from human understanding—which the Talmud calls 'what is above, what is below'—had become depressed and gloomy. As a result, despite his great wealth, he was consumed by an irrational fear of death. Wherever he turned, it seemed to him that he saw the Angel of Death striding toward him with his unsheathed sword in his hand.

"Due to his dread and depression, he became sickly and had trouble walking. But what really caused him pain and anguish was seeing Reb Abish the Hasid, the pauper who had not a kopeck to his name, walking around town radiating joy, almost dancing from his pleasure and delight in life, as if he had won the top prize in the lottery! The rich man seethed with hatred and resentment for the Hasid. He despised him and plotted his revenge, either to harm him or to have him kicked out of town.

"On weekdays, when he was involved in his business and other matters, Reb Getzel was somewhat calm. But on Sabbaths and holidays, when the two met in the synagogue and Reb Getzel saw how lively and joyful Reb Abish was and how his face radiated happiness, Reb Getzel would almost go into shock. To the same extent that the Hasid was immersed in a joy that steadily increased and deepened, the rich man was consumed and overcome by anger, depression, sadness, and fear.

"But a rich man is still a rich man, and as the Torah says, 'a wealthy man will speak haughtily' and strike terror into the hearts of poor common people who depend on him for their livelihood and in countless other ways. Despite themselves, they become his friends and allies, to side with him and do his bidding. When the townspeople saw that the rich man despised the Hasid and was persecuting him, they also persecuted him, even though in their hearts they respected and revered him. They wanted to find favor with the rich man and to benefit from his patronage. What else could they do? After all, the need to eat can cause a person to transgress!

"When the festival of Sukkot approached and the Hasid needed boards to build his *sukkah,* suddenly and mysteriously, all the boards in the town disappeared.

Wherever Reb Abish went to ask for boards, they gave him one answer: 'There are no boards.'

"Reb Abish the Hasid realized that Reb Getzel was behind this evil business. 'What do I care!' he whispered to himself, lifting his eyes to heaven. 'Everything that God does is for good! If it is His will, then I won't build my own *sukkah.* Other good Jews will invite me into their *sukkahs.* God willing, I won't remain outside!'

"But the rich man had decided otherwise. He made sure that everyone in town knew that he would retaliate against anyone who let Reb Abish into his *sukkah* on the holiday. And he had word passed to Reb Abish that if he did not want to be humiliated and insulted by not being invited into other people's *sukkahs,* and if he did not want to fail to fulfill the main *mitzvah* of the holiday, to be in a *sukkah*—and what could be worse to a truly pious man?—he had two choices: either to stop being so happy or to leave town!

"But Reb Abish did not lose hope and he would not so easily give up his happiness! 'Happiness is the foundation of divine service,' he said to himself, 'and all Hasidic teaching is based on it! The Torah itself warns that the whole *Tochachah* [Rebuke; the section of curses pronounced in Deuteronomy against Israel's disobedience] came as a punishment 'because you did not serve the Lord your God with joy and gladness of heart.' And in any case, how is it possible to live without joy? A famous holy book says that one of the reasons for the *mitzvah* 'to rejoice in your holiday' is that 'a person, by his very nature, needs to rejoice occasionally, just as he needs food, rest, and sleep.' So how can I give up my joy and happiness? But as for having a *sukkah*, God will help!'

"Lost in these thoughts, Reb Abish trod the streets, not realizing that he had reached the outskirts of town and the Jewish cemetery beyond the last dwellings.

"Paltiel, the cemetery caretaker and gravedigger, hated Getzel the Rich Man, who arrogantly struck fear into the hearts of the townspeople. But although everyone was afraid of Getzel, Paltiel knew that in the end, Getzel too would fall into his hands—and into one of his graves!

"Paltiel had heard of the disgusting plot against Reb Abish the Hasid, the dearest of men, to prevent him from fulfilling the *mitzvah* to erect a *sukkah*, simply because of his only 'sin' of being pious, making do with little, and always being joyful! Why had all the townspeople shunned him and given in to the threats of that depressed and miserable madman Getzel?

"Paltiel went over and greeted Reb Abish and whispered in his ear, 'Go home, Reb Abish. Don't worry. You'll have boards for a *sukkah*. You'll fulfill the *mitzvah* of building a *sukkah*, and you'll be happy and joyful until a hundred and twenty years!' From whom better to receive the traditional blessing of a long life than a gravedigger?

"By the time Reb Abish returned home from his walk, boards for a *sukkah* were already waiting for him there—supplied by Paltiel, who had driven to Reb Abish's home in his wagon! Where did Paltiel get them? Today," explained Rabbi Aharon Asher as he told his story, "grave markers are made from stone, expensive marble, and people pay extravagant sums of money for them, but in former times, most grave markers were made of wood. A gravedigger had a supply of boards, finished or unfinished, each one rounded off on top, where was engraved the Hebrew abbreviation for the words 'Here lies' followed by a blank space; when they wanted to put up a marker on the grave of a deceased person, they filled in his name.

"When Paltiel the Gravedigger brought the boards to Reb Abish's house, it was already the eve of the holiday. Reb Abish quickly built his *sukkah* with the letters for 'Here lies' to the outside, and he was confident that sitting inside the *sukkah*–and not seeing the troubling abbreviation–he would be able to rejoice fully, as one should, as the Torah says about rejoicing on Sukkot, 'and you should be *only* joyful'–without the least trace of worry or sadness!

"Getzel the Rich Man, certain that the Hasid was without a *sukkah* and therefore miserable, went out on the first day of the holiday to take a walk around town, to find the Hasid and savor his revenge. But how great was his shock and dismay when, walking among the many *sukkahs* in town, he heard bursting from one of them the joyous sounds of a Sukkot holiday song: 'And you should be only joyful . . . *only joyful!*' When he recognized Reb Abish the Hasid's voice, Reb Getzel's anger burned within him. His jealousy was so great he felt he would go insane–that that pauper of a Hasid is still happy while he is miserable! He was even more enraged that one of the Jews in town had betrayed him and given boards to Reb Abish!

"He wanted to run away before Reb Abish the Hasid realized he was there, but his desire to know who had supplied the boards to his enemy overcame him. He arrogantly burst in to Reb Abish's *sukkah* and, without even a greeting, shrieked, 'Where did you get these boards?'

"Reb Abish, instead of becoming confused or frightened or feeling humiliated, smiled warmly and radiantly at his uninvited guest and greeted him with 'Happy holiday!' Then he quietly stood up, went outside, and pointed to the Hebrew abbreviation for 'Here lies' on the boards of his *sukkah*. 'Do you see where these boards came from, Reb Getzel?'

"The moment the rich man saw the letters and understood their meaning, he was so stunned and bewildered that he almost collapsed. A dark dread and a fear of death came over him. It seemed to him that he saw the Angel of Death standing in front of him.

"'Be calm, Reb Getzel,' said Reb Abish, 'and let me tell you what happened.

"'I was walking on the street earlier today, with one thought on my mind: Where can I get boards for a *sukkah*? Everyone I asked told me, "We have no boards. None!" Suddenly, I saw the Angel of Death walking toward me. "What are you doing in our town?" I asked, "Whose soul have you come to take?"

"'"I'm here to take the soul of Getzel the Rich Man," he replied, "to have revenge on him for the arrogant and repulsive way he's treated you! Who has ever heard of such a thing, to punish a poor Jew for the 'sin' of being joyful and trusting in God? Should it surprise anyone that this rich man is terrified of death and depressed? He has no fear of God! He's no privileged character to me! To me, rich and poor are perfectly equal: here today; tomorrow in the grave!'"

"When the rich man heard Reb Abish's story, he almost fainted; his face turned white, his teeth began to chatter, and he began to tremble like a leaf.

"'But I'm still alive!' he stammered.

"'Of course you're alive!' said Reb Abish, 'Because I didn't let him go to get you! I didn't want another Jew to be punished for my sake. I said to the Angel of Death, "If another Jew does wrong, does that mean I should do wrong also? God forbid! The Torah says, 'You shall not take revenge or bear a grudge.' And doesn't the Talmud say, 'A person doesn't stub his toe on earth unless it has been decreed in heaven'? Any pain I suffered was decreed in heaven. Even if Getzel did wrong, he was only an agent—and God has many agents, although He brings about evil through evil people and good through good people. So why should I be angry at Getzel and blame him? Furthermore," I argued, "if Reb Getzel died, what would happen to the town's Jews whose livelihood depends on him? Even if he's wicked, as you say, it's still not a good enough reason to take his soul, because the Rabbis say that the wicked are called dead even while alive, so he's dead anyway! Rebbe Aharon of Karlin said that depression is hell itself. If Getzel is already being punished while alive, why are you taking his soul?"

""If that's what you want," said the Angel of Death, "I'll spare him. I only wanted to help you."

""Leave Reb Getzel alone!" I said. "Don't harm him! But if you wanted to do me a favor, I have a favor to ask you: I need boards for a *sukkah*! Can you get them for me?"

""I have a good idea," answered the Angel of Death. "I have a friend in town, he's almost a member of my family—Paltiel the Gravedigger—and he has a big supply of boards for grave markers. I'm sure he'll gladly lend you some, if I recommend you to him. You can use them to make a fine *sukkah*."

"'That was what happened, Reb Getzel. Paltiel the Gravedigger brought me the boards, and as you see, thank God, I'm happily fulfilling the *mitzvah* to dwell in a *sukkah*. But listen to me, Reb Getzel, why don't you change the ways that make you miserable and start to have faith and trust in God, and together we'll fulfill God's *mitzvah*—"and you shall rejoice before the Lord your God"—"and you should be only joyful."'

"While he was still speaking, Reb Abish took hold of Reb Getzel's hands and began to hum and then sing until he began dancing fervently, leading Getzel around after him. *A-n-d y-o-u s-h-o-u-l-d b-e o-n-l-y j-o-y-f-u-l, o-n-l-y j-o-y-f-u-l!*

"Reb Getzel could not resist the Hasid's joy. He felt as if he was becoming another person: his depression

disappeared into the air, and joy and happiness filled
his heart. He felt happier than he had ever been in his
life. His fear at life left him, and in its place came a
peaceful confidence and elevated thoughts about the
joy of being alive. Suddenly, he remembered that it was
a holiday and he should rejoice. Feeling a powerful
urge to do just that, he remembered the saying of Rebbe
Aharon of Karlin that Reb Abish the Hasid had once
told him: that pure and holy thoughts come only
from joy."[10]

When Rabbi Aharon Asher ended his tale, with
its obvious lesson, he joyfully called out a blessing to
his fellow Hasidim sitting in his *sukkah:* "May we all
rejoice next year in Jerusalem and sit in a *sukkah*
together with the Messiah!"[11] Then he closed his eyes
and lifted his voice in a Hasidic melody, as he did after
every tale he told. His voice, which had a special grace,
was so sweet to his friends' ears that their emotions
were overwhelmed and they were irresistibly drawn
in to join in his song. Their singing soon became
powerful and passionate, and before long, they all
began dancing in the *sukkah*, holding hands, then link-
ing arms, until the tide of their ecstatic fervor swelled
so that they were actually close to passing from this
world.[12] ❧

Rabbi Aharon Asher, like Reb Abish in the story, was truly joyful and brought joy to others. He not only told stories but also lived
their teachings. And he knew the secret of mystic joy.

Simhat Torah *Joy on Yom Kippur*

At the beginning of the Jewish religious calendar, there is a long series of holidays and special observances: First, there is *Selihot,* the early-morning penitential prayers recited during the week leading up to Rosh HaShanah, the Jewish New Year, when Jews rededicate themselves to a religious life. Rosh HaShanah initiates the Ten Days of Repentance that conclude with Yom Kippur, the Day of Atonement. Yom Kippur is followed after a few days by Sukkot, commemorating the ancient Jews' sojourn in the Sinai Desert when they dwelt in booths. And all these holidays conclude with Simhat Torah, celebrating the "Joy of the Torah," when Jews rejoice at the divine gift of God's Word.

Yom Kippur is a solemn day of fasting and repentance, a time to reflect on one's spiritual condition and to ask God and people you have offended during the year to forgive your sins. Simhat Torah, by contrast, is a very joyous holiday, when Jews dance exuberantly in the synagogue and sometimes outside on the street with Torah scrolls.

⊷ Once, on the day before Yom Kippur, a Jewish innkeeper living near Berditchev—the town of Rebbe Levi Yitzhak of Berditchev—was arrested by the landowner from whom he rented his inn.

The innkeeper had not paid his rent in a very long time. He simply did not have the money. Business was poor, and he had a large family. What could he do?

Now in those days, each landowning lord had great authority, like a king, with the power of life and death over the peasants and Jews living on his territory. When an innkeeper—and most of the innkeepers were Jewish—could not pay his rent, he and his family were thrown into a pit, a dungeon, and left there until someone paid their debt. If no one helped them, they would stay there indefinitely to suffer and starve to death.

After the landowner had threatened and warned this innkeeper to pay his rent and waited for a number of days to see if he could raise the money, he threw the man and his family into prison on the day before Yom Kippur. He then informed the Jewish community that unless they paid the overdue rent—three hundred rubles, no small sum in those days—the family would rot in the dungeon where he had put them.

The Rabbis teach that redeeming captives is one of the Torah's greatest commandments. So one of the Hasidim in Berditchev took it upon himself to collect the money to redeem this family. Although the sum involved was well beyond his own means, he was determined to raise the money somehow, because he knew that the lives of the family depended on it. They had no one else to help them, and if he was unable to collect the money, they would remain where they were, with possibly fatal consequences. He had decided to do anything necessary to free the family before Yom Kippur—how could one leave a Jewish family in prison on the holiest day of the year?

He began collecting. Since it was the day before Yom Kippur, people were sympathetic and gave generously. But they did not give enough—not because they did not want to but because they simply did not have enough to give! After collecting for several hours, the Hasid had managed to gather only fifty rubles.

He knew he needed three hundred rubles, and he realized that at this pace, he would never get the money before Yom Kippur; in fact, he was worried that he might not get the money at all. He decided to take a rasher course of action and headed to the neighborhood where the more assimilated Jews lived. These were mostly younger people who worked with the non-Jewish landlords. They were wealthier but usually less religious and less concerned about the welfare of their fellow Jews. Still, it was the day before Yom Kippur, and there could be no better time to approach them.

When he reached that neighborhood, the Hasid went to a tavern where these young Jewish men spent much of their time. He entered and found a large hall filled with people who were sitting at tables gambling at cards and drinking liquor. The fact that in a few hours, Jews all over the world would begin reciting *Kol Nidrei*, the first prayer of the Yom Kippur evening service, did not appear to affect them.

The Hasid saw that the tables were covered with money for their gambling. On any one of the tables, there was enough money to redeem the family. He approached one group of card players and said, "My friends, tonight is Yom Kippur, the one day when God forgives everyone. Why not prepare for the day? I have something constructive for you to do with your money: a Jewish family is in terrible need; they are in prison for debt. Instead of wasting your money gambling, please, give it away for a good purpose!"

At first, the men just ignored him. But the Hasid was persistent. Finally, one of them said to him, "You know what? You see the vodka standing here on the table? It's *finif un nineṡiker.*" In Yiddish, *finif un nineṡiker* means "ninety-five." The bottle was 95 percent alcohol—that is not 95 proof, it is 190 proof. The man filled an ordinary drinking glass and told him, "If you drink a glass of this *finif un nineṡiker,* we'll give you a hundred rubles for your cause from our table alone."

The Hasid's gut reaction was, "How can I drink a glass of vodka that's 190 proof? *Kol Nidrei* is a couple of hours away! After a full glass of this, I'll be finished. There's no way I'll be able to concentrate on my prayers." But then a second thought came to him: "If they give me a hundred rubles, I'll have a third of the amount I need to save this family. What should I be more concerned with? Having a better Yom Kippur myself, or doing everything I can to save the family? Who knows how long it will take to collect one hundred rubles any other way?" So he decided to drink the glass of vodka.

He downed the glass, and the gamblers had a laugh, but they kept their word and gave him the money. He wobbled over to the next table and spoke to the card players there. "Your friends just gave me a hundred rubles to help a poor family in prison for debt. Why not do the same?"

"You know what?" the men said, "We'll do the same, but you'll have to do the same too. If you drink another glass of *finif un nineʒiker*, we'll give you one hundred rubles too."

The Hasid began to plead with them. "Please, tonight is *Kol Nidrei*. As it is, I'm going to be dizzy during the prayers; but if I drink another glass, I'll just be out. If you're going to give me the money anyway, why make me do this?"

But they demanded their entertainment. "Listen, either you drink it or good-bye." Again, the Hasid thought, "Which is more important: my Yom Kippur or getting this family out of the dungeon earlier?" He did not have to think long. He knew the answer. So he gave them their entertainment and drank the glass of vodka. They laughed, but they gave him the hundred rubles, and everybody was happy.

Then he wobbled over to a third table and asked whether the players would contribute to the cause. Since he had started with fifty rubles, he explained to them that now he needed less than a hundred rubles. It was just hours before Yom Kippur, and they could make it possible for a poor family to spend the holiday outside a dungeon.

They were not interested in his explanations, but they were prepared to continue the fun. So they made him the same offer: one hundred rubles for a glass of *finif un nineʒiker*. He did not have to think much at all. Particularly after two glasses of vodka, it was very clear to him: "Forget about your Yom Kippur; think about the family. With this glass you can get them out today." He drank the third glass, and they gave him the hundred rubles. Now he had all the money he needed to get the family out of prison.

He asked the gamblers a favor. "Please, can someone help me get to the home of this landowner so that I can give him the money?" He was in no condition to go there himself. The spirit of Yom Kippur must have been in the air, for one of the gamblers excused himself from his friends and drove the Hasid to the landowner's home in his carriage, after which he returned to the tavern and his card playing.

The landowner was not happy to see this drunken Hasid at his door, but he was delighted to get his three hundred rubles. After counting the money, he ordered that the family be released. Of course, they were overcome with joy. The landowner told them that this Hasid had freed them, and after learning who their savior was, the innkeeper ran over to the Hasid and hugged him, thanking him again and again. The whole family was crying. But the Hasid was not interested in receiving thanks. He did not see anything special in what he had done. He gave the man the fifty extra rubles to buy food and other needs for his family. Then he asked him one favor: "I won't be able to get to the synagogue by myself. Can you help me get there?"

Needless to say, the innkeeper took the unsteady Hasid to the synagogue. There the Hasid lay down on one of the benches. He knew that he would not be able to pray, but he wanted to at least sleep in the holy atmosphere of the synagogue on Yom Kippur.

Soon people started coming to the synagogue for *Kol Nidrei.* Before the services began, everyone took a psalm book in hand and began to pray. As the din of their prayers began to rise, the Hasid woke up groggily from his stupor. Looking out the window with blurred vision and seeing that it was night and looking around in the synagogue and seeing all the Torah scrolls being taken from the Ark, he assumed, as a drunken person might, that it was Simhat Torah, for then too the Torah scrolls are all taken out at night! So already in a happy mood from the vodka, he jumped up, ran over to someone holding a Torah, took it from him, and began to dance.

The other congregants were shocked at the sight. Was he drunk? Was he crazy? What was going on? To dance like this on Yom Kippur, the most solemn day of the year! Some of them rushed to take the Torah from him and kick him out of the synagogue, but just then the Berditchever Rebbe, who was at the prayer leader's stand, turned around and called out, "Stop! Leave him alone!" for, before the innkeeper—who was of course in bad shape and not able to attend services—had gone home, he had told the rebbe what the Hasid had done.

The Berditchever and the whole congregation watched as the Hasid danced in blissful oblivion for a few minutes. Then, when they saw that he was about to conk out again, they rushed over, steadied him, took the Torah scroll from him, and laid him down gently on a bench, where he quickly went to sleep again.

The Berditchever said to his astonished congregation, "My friends, this Hasid had a reason to dance today." After telling them why the Hasid had gotten drunk and given up his Yom Kippur to save a Jewish family from prison, the rebbe continued, "The holidays at this time of year are actually all connected to each other. First, comes Selihot, which leads into Rosh HaShanah and the Ten Days of Repentance, and they lead into Yom Kippur. After Yom Kippur comes Sukkot, the "season of our rejoicing," and finally, the chain of holidays concludes with Simhat Torah, when we celebrate and dance with God's Torah.

"Why is Simhat Torah the culmination of all the holidays? Because joy is the highest worship there is. This Hasid is not missing Yom Kippur because of his selfless deed," said the Berditchever. "He simply skipped over it and entered immediately into the joy of Simhat Torah."[13] ⋘⋙

Rejoicing at Your Brother's Simha

⋘⋙ Rebbe Naftali of Ropshitz used to happily recount a teaching about Simhat Torah that he received from a simple Jew, a porter.

Rebbe Naftali once saw how this porter, who was completely ignorant of the Torah, was singing and dancing like crazy on Simhat Torah. Rebbe Naftali called him over and said, "Why are you dancing and rejoicing so much? Have you studied so much Torah this year that you're so happy?"

The man answered, "Rebbe! If my brother has a *simha*, a family celebration, don't I rejoice and dance with him?"[14] ⋙

A person's joy in Judaism, in God, does not depend on his being learned, holy, or saintly. He can rejoice that he is related to this whole awesome project called Judaism. He can dance, knowing that there were and are other Jews who have reached higher than he has, who have reached even the highest spiritual levels.

The unlearned porter meant that a fellow Jew, like Rebbe Naftali, who had studied and was learned, was indeed his "brother" and he could also rejoice with him and with the Torah. Every Jew can share in the joy of his fellow Jews and what they have attained, and every Jew can rejoice because he too has a mystic connection to the Torah that reaches beyond what he knows or has studied.

The Baal Shem Tov About Joy on Tu BeShvat

⋙ Once, on Tu BeShvat, the Baal Shem Tov was sitting with his closest disciples in Medzibuz. They were eating fruits in honor of the day, drinking *"L'hayim!"*–To life!– and discussing the importance of joy. During this conversation, the Baal Shem Tov said, "Joy is so great, because by joy a person can reach an exalted spiritual level so that he sees the *Shechinah.* After the verse 'You shall be only joyful,' the Torah continues, 'Three times a year, every man of you shall be seen [appear in the Temple] before the presence of the Lord your God.'[15] When a Jew is happy, he is revealing that he is satisfied with the world that the Holy One, blessed be He, has created and

also with the behavior of all the Children of Israel, the
people close to Him. He has no complaints against
heaven and no demands or grievances against any other
Jew. Everything is good, upright, acceptable, fitting, and
sweet, and this kind of joy, which brings a person to
have a good eye, so that he looks on the Creator and His
creatures lovingly, causes a revelation of the *Shechinah*.
That is the secret of the teaching of our Sages, who said
about the person who goes to the Temple to 'be seen' by
God: 'Just as he came to be seen, so does he come to
see'—that is, to see the Divine Presence."

After this conversation about joy, the Baal Shem
Tov suggested to his Hasidim that they go out for a
sleigh ride together in the snow-covered countryside
and take along with them some wine, honey cake,
whiskey, and fruits for Tu BeShvat.

As they careened along in the sleigh, the snow was
falling and they were so joyful that they felt they were
lifted up on a cloud of light. Remembering that it was Tu
BeShvat, they sang songs from the kabbalistic Book of
Song, *Perek Shira*, that explains which Torah verses animals and plants "sing" praising their Creator. They sang,
"The fig tree says, 'The one who tends the fig tree shall
eat its fruit.' The pomegranate says, 'Your cheeks are like
the halves of a pomegranate.' The palm tree says, 'A righteous person shall flourish like a palm tree.'"

The road entered the forest, and the horses gal-
loped in pleasure, kicking up snow all over. On the two
sides of the road, an ancient, dense forest stretched out
with trees whose branches leaned out, arching over the

road, almost touching in the middle and nearly block-
ing out the sunlight. But here and there the sun peeked
through the branches, lighting the travelers' path as
they sped along in the sleigh. And as they went, they
sang another song from the Book of Song: "Then shall
the trees of the forest sing for joy before the Lord . . . !"

Their singing grew stronger and stronger, and
flocks of birds flying above them began chirping so
loudly that it seemed that they were singing along with
the joyful travelers in the sleigh.[16] ≪◈≫

The Baal Shem Tov and his disciples knew the secret—that God
is within the world. How could they not sing? When we too know that
secret, we too will sing and will hear the songs of the trees and the
birds praising God.

The Dance of Tu BeShvat

≪◈≫ It was Tu BeShvat in the year 1943, during the
Second World War. Tens of thousands of forlorn Polish-
Jewish refugees, fleeing the Nazi invasion of Russia,
gathered in the far reaches of the Soviet Union—in
Samarkand. Of all the war refugees there, the lot of the
Jews was the worst. Who would pity them? Who would
extend to them a brotherly hand or favor them with a
compassionate look?

But then suddenly there appeared a good angel in
the form of Rabbi Rafael of the Jewish community of
Bukhara. He had all the virtues of a tzaddik, but above
all he was dedicated to emulating the hospitality of

Abraham. Rabbi Rafael's house, which his family had owned for many generations, had a very spacious courtyard. It was a miracle that the Communists had not expropriated this house from him. But even the "Red Commissars" treated the gentle and pure Rabbi Rafael respectfully. In any case, the Jews who were uprooted, outcast, and homeless streamed through the gates into his large courtyard. And there, with Rabbi Rafael, they found a refuge and a sanctuary; they found help and support.

Rabbi Rafael always had a smiling face; whenever a new visitor arrived—a sad and suffering refugee—he was greeted warmly. Rabbi Rafael's face glowed even more on Sabbaths and holidays, when he wore his colorful Bukharan robe. But anyone who had not seen the light shining from his face on Tu BeShvat had never seen holy joy in his life. Why did Rabbi Rafael rejoice so on Tu BeShvat? There were two reasons.

First of all, there were a number of fruit trees growing in Rabbi Rafael's courtyard. Since the winter in Samarkand leaves early and spring enters quickly, these fruit trees were already beginning to show the first signs of blossoms on Tu BeShvat. It is a *mitzvah* when first seeing trees blossom in the spring to recite a special blessing—"Blessed art Thou, O Lord our God, King of the universe, whose world lacks nothing and who created beautiful creatures and trees to benefit and delight human beings." So it was possible for Rabbi Rafael to make blessings over these blossoming trees in honor of the New Year, the Rosh HaShanah of the

Trees, as these blessings appear in the ancient prayer books of the Bukharan Jews. Therefore, his joy overflowed on Tu BeShvat.

But the second and perhaps the main reason for his happiness is that among Rabbi Rafael's fruit trees was an apricot tree. Apricot trees also grow in the Holy Land, which was not true of the other trees that belonged to him. Therefore, the apricot tree was precious to him because it reminded him of the Land of Israel. So when Rabbi Rafael would see the apricot tree blossoming, his joy was boundless. The dream of his life, to see the Holy Land with his own eyes, sprouted anew right in front of him on that day.

When Rabbi Rafael felt his heart fill with joy, he invited every refugee who had taken shelter with him to be outside in the shade of the fruit trees that were waking up from their frozen winter slumber; he gathered all his guests into his courtyard in honor of the Holiday of the Trees. Rabbi Rafael's joy was limitless. But how could he draw into his happiness and overflowing joy all those crushed and broken Jews, whose whole world had been destroyed?

He found a way. He said to the refugees, "Look at the trees blossoming! A few weeks ago, they were barren and bare, in the throes of winter! I tell you, our winter too will end!" Then he took out from a hidden spot two bags of raisins and almonds. The refugees could not believe their eyes. Raisins and almonds in the midst of this war and famine?

Rabbi Rafael walked about his courtyard and, his eyes gleaming with affection, gave a generous handful of raisins and almonds to every refugee. That did the miracle.

Those who were sorrowful revived all at once when they felt the raisins and almonds between their fingers. When the good smell reach their nostrils, it reminded them of all the good things they had once had, and it gave them hope for the future. It was like a gust of wind with good news from a world that once was and now had been destroyed. So they began to revive. Rabbi Rafael made a blessing in honor of Tu BeShvat over the raisins and almonds.

Then he went and got his special treat: some dried apricots from the previous year. He always made the *shehecheyanu* blessing for having reached "this auspicious time" over an apricot from his own tree. "Blessed art Thou . . . who hast kept us in life, and sustained us, and enabled us to reach this season!" he called out in his booming voice.

Then Rabbi Rafael melted in joy and began to dance in stormy ecstasy. He sang and danced in the courtyard in honor of the holiday. His eyes were raised to heaven, and his heart was directed far away eastward to the Holy Land. As he chewed the apricot with eyes closed, he inwardly promised himself to one day see the Land of Israel and enjoy its fruits. Rabbi Rafael was dancing in Samarkand, but his heart was in Jerusalem.

The homeless and hapless Jewish refugees made
the blessing of *shehecheyanu*. Then they joined in with
Rabbi Rafael's singing and danced with him in a circle
until their legs were swept away in the joyous current
of the dance. That is how Samarkand danced in honor of
Tu BeShvat.[17] ⋘

How Joy and Love Can Conquer Hate

The first two of the three tales in this section relate to the holidays of Purim and Passover. Purim falls in the Hebrew month of Adar and is followed in the next month of Nisan by Passover. Both holidays celebrate miraculous deliverances, although the deliverances were different from each other.

On Purim, Jews celebrate their escape from the extermination plotted against them in ancient Persia by the wicked Haman. The heroes of the redemption were Mordechai and his niece Esther. This deliverance is commemorated yearly by a number of observances, such as the reading of the *Megillah*, the scroll of the Book of Esther, which tells the Purim story, and a feast that takes place on the day of the holiday in the late afternoon. A peculiar Purim custom is that during the feast, Jews are obligated to become intoxicated *ad d'lo yada*—"until they no longer know the difference between 'blessed is Mordechai' and 'cursed is Haman.'" They must drink until they cannot distinguish a saintly Jew from a genocidal antisemite! This custom is part of the "carnival" atmosphere of Purim, when everything is turned upside down and mockery and fun are the order of the day.

On Passover, Jews sit around the festive *seder* table and recite the *Haggadah,* the ancient story of their ancestors' exodus from Egypt. The Passover table is laden with wine, *matzah*—the unleavened bread the Jews ate as they fled Egypt—and other symbolic foods. At

the beginning of the *seder,* a child chants the Four Questions about
the unusual foods and customs of Passover. The first question, which
in Hebrew begins *Mah Nishtana . . . ,* is "Why is this night different
from all other nights?" The parent or leader then recites the answers.
At one point, everyone present recites the words from the *Haggadah*
that each Jew should see himself as having been redeemed from slavery, for during the *seder* ceremony, each participant is supposed to
relive ancient events and transcend his own slavery to personal limitations on his spirituality.

All Jewish holidays are attempts to reawaken the special energy that characterizes the day so that each individual can internal-
ize the holiday's spiritual teaching and apply its lessons.

Purim and Passover are both paths to a personal redemption
that leads to joy.

Rebbe David of Dinov Celebrates Purim

The Torah tells how in the desert, shortly after the exodus from Egypt,
the tribe of Amalek mercilessly attacked the defenseless Jewish strag-
glers. In retribution, the Torah commands the Jewish people to wipe
out Amalek, but this has long been understood in a purely symbolic
way; there are no more Amalekites today, and no physical destruction
is intended for anyone. "Wiping out Amalek" is understood spiritually
to mean removing the part of one's psyche that attempts to cool off
one's religious ardor. According to Jewish tradition, wicked Haman,
the Purim villain, was a descendant of the tribe of Amalek.

᠅ Rebbe David of Dinov was once celebrating the
Purim feast in the synagogue with his Hasidim; it had
started in the late afternoon and continued with full
strength into the evening. They were all enjoying the
food and drinking liquor, as is customary. The musicians were playing, the Hasidim were singing and danc-

ing, and joy reigned supreme until, in their holy inebriation, they no longer knew the difference between
"blessed is Mordechai" and "cursed is Haman." It was
as if there was no more evil in the world, as if everything was holy, everything was good.

But even though they were joyful, one problem
was on everyone's mind. There was a rumor that some
of the gentiles in Dinov were planning a pogrom that
was to take place a month hence—on Passover, when
pogroms were often carried out by drunken peasants
incited by their priests. It was said that the pogrom
would be on the first night of Passover, when all the
Jews would be in their homes, celebrating the *seder.*
In fact, Rebbe David had heard that these antisemites
were meeting right then in a tavern on the gentile side
of town to plan their evil deeds.

About midnight, Rebbe David said to his Hasidim
at the table, "We've done something right here in the
synagogue to wipe out Amalek. But do you want to
finish the job? To really wipe out Amalek?"

The Hasidim called back, "Yes, Rebbe, we're ready!"

"If your answer is yes," said Rebbe David, "then sing
and dance with me now with all your heart and soul!"

The rebbe led the Hasidim in a joyous song, and
they danced with ecstatic abandon. They sang the Hasidic melody over and over until everyone present had
entered fully—with head, hands, feet, and even boots—
into the supernal realm of joy.

In the midst of this exuberant and elated singing
and dancing, which carried everyone present to the

heights of joyous ecstasy, the rebbe suddenly called out, "The time has come. Let's go!" He got up and led the Hasidim and the musicians outside the synagogue, and they all piled into wagons and started riding through the streets—with the musicians playing and the Hasidim singing—right into the gentile neighborhood.

Dinov was a tiny town; they reached the gentile neighborhood in a few minutes. The rebbe had them drive right up to the tavern where the antisemites were doing their plotting, and the Hasidim climbed down from the wagons and followed the rebbe into the tavern, all of them singing and dancing in joyous abandon.

The peasants were by this time a little drunk and had begun to curse the Jews. But just then Rebbe David walked in the door, holy and pure and shining like an angel of God. He walked right up to the leader of the antisemites, took his hand, and started to dance with him. Then each Hasid took the hand of an antisemite, and they all began to dance in great joy. The whole room became filled with holiness and sweetness.

After an hour or two of singing and dancing, they sat down to rest, and all the peasants and Hasidim crowded around Rebbe David. Turning to the peasants, he said, "My dearest brothers, there's something I must ask you. I'm so happy to be with you, and I'm so glad I came. But I have to tell you: I heard that you hate Jews! Is there somebody here that hates us?"

The leader of the antisemites, looking down at his feet, shook his head in denial and said embarrassedly, "No, that's not true!" All the peasants looked around at one another, and each one said, "Not me! Maybe someone else; I don't hate Jews!"

"I've heard an unbelievable rumor–though I'm sure it's not true!–that you were planning a pogrom against us," said the rebbe.

"Not us!" said the leader, looking around evasively and blushing with shame at his fellow plotters.

"If that's so," said Rebbe David, "then why shouldn't we be the best of friends?"

All the peasants were so moved by the rebbe's holiness and love that they all shouted out, "Yes, Rebbe, yes! Be our best friend!"

Then the real dancing began.[1] ⋘⋙

The obligation to become drunk on Purim until one no longer knows the difference between "blessed is Mordechai" and "cursed is Haman" has a mystical meaning. On Purim, Jews are to use liquor to help them rise to that transcendent mystic level where one sees that all humans, the wicked as well as the good, both Haman and Mordechai, are part of God's plan, for the divine drama cannot proceed without the villain to move the action forward. From this elevated spiritual perspective, Jews realize that, at least sometimes, they may be able to overcome their enemies not by might, not by power, but by the holy spirit of love and joy.

"Amalek" exists externally in the form of antisemites, but the Sages say that Amalek also exists internally, within the breast of each Jew, as an aspect of his "evil inclination," particularly that part that tells one it is fine to be religious but urges one not to "overdo it." One way to extirpate that evil impulse is by rising above it to a level of devotion and divine joy where one no longer desires evil and can no longer be affected by it at all. Some mystics say a similar tactic can also, at least sometimes, conquer external evil—wicked people. One can wipe out Amalek not by physically destroying people but by attaining a divine joy that lifts one above any enmity and hatred and turns one's own heart and then even theirs to love.

Judaism often takes what is secular and makes it sacred. For example, Hasidim particularly use liquor to arouse their religious emotions. This is true of the carnival aspect of Purim, when drunkenness is used to induce a state of holy looseness and joy. In this tale, the antisemites drank liquor in their tavern and the Hasidim drank liquor in their synagogue. But whereas secular drinking opens the heart to either love or hate, Hasidic drinking opens it only to love. Just as the Hasidim use liquor for a religious purpose, they sometimes, in a similar way, take secular gentile drinking songs and convert them into holy songs by interpreting the words in a spiritual way, as in the next tale.

A Prison Seder

◈ At the beginning of World War II, in Poland, a Hasidic rebbe was arrested by the Nazis and put in a prison cell with a mixed group of Jews and Poles. The Poles were common criminals—thieves, pimps, and so on. The Jews had been arrested for political activities—for putting out an underground newspaper in the ghetto, for trying to escape the ghetto by jumping over the wall, or for being on the street after the special curfew for Jews. Others had been arrested for studying Torah or for gathering to pray. Some had no idea why they were in prison.

The rebbe, who had been arrested for refusing to cease from his religious activities, prayed quietly with great devotion and fervor, three times every day, in the corner of the cell. All the Jews respected him greatly, and he radiated an inner peace, joy, and confidence that come only from the deepest faith.

One night after having spent several days in prison, the rebbe, who wanted to share his faith and joy with his fellow Jews, who were deeply depressed, said, "Jews! Why are you so sad? Don't you know tonight is the first night of Passover? Don't we have to celebrate? This night is different from all other nights! We have no wine or matzah, but we can still recite the *Haggadah.* I know it by heart. Come, sit by me and we'll say it together."

Some of the Jews said, "Rebbe, how can we celebrate our freedom from Egyptian slavery when we're slaves to the Nazis? We're slaves now, today!"

"In the *Haggadah,*" replied the rebbe, "it says, 'This year we are here; next year may we be in the Land of Israel! This year we are slaves; next year may we be free people!' You are a slave only if you give up your hope to be free, if you admit to being a slave and accept it! We Jews can never be slaves because we won't admit to it. We are servants only to the Holy One, blessed be He!"

The Jews, some of whom were religious and others of whom were not, were all inspired by the rebbe's words and by his faith and confidence. They called out, "Yes, yes, the rebbe's right!"

So they came over and sat close around the rebbe as he began to recite the *Haggadah.* Although they had no candles, matzah, wine, or any food, they could still have their *seder.* The rebbe said, "We don't have anything over which to ask the *Mah Nishtana,* the Four Questions [because they are asked about the symbolic foods on the *seder* plate], so we'll start with the answer, *Avadim Hayinu,* 'We were Slaves to Pharaoh in Egypt.'" And he began to chant the *Haggadah.* When the others remembered parts of it or when the rebbe sang a *niggun,* a melody, they joined in with him.

Suddenly, one of the Polish criminals, a thief and low-life, began to yell. "You filthy Jews, what are you doing? Do you think this is a synagogue here? You're making me sick with your prayers! Shut up!" And he began to call to the Nazi guard, "These Jews are turning this place into a synagogue. Shut them up!"

The Nazi guard came running in and, when the Pole complained to him, said, "You dirty Jews better shut up or you'll pay for your singing!" Then he said to the Pole, "Thank you so much for helping me with these miserable Jews. I'm putting you in charge of them. If they step out of line again, call me, and I'll take care of them." Then he left.

While the Nazi was yelling and threatening, the rebbe showed not the slightest fear. He was not intimidated at all. But now, after the Nazi left, he began to weep, and tears ran down his cheeks. He was weeping because of his pity for the Pole who had called the Nazi guard. The rebbe, who spoke Polish, said to him, "I'm so sad for you; how low you've sunk! Don't you have any character left? Woe to the person who willingly makes himself a slave to the wicked! The Nazis consider you Poles like dogs, and you side with them against us? Don't you see that we're in this together?"

The other Poles, who had been watching and listening, suddenly became animated and nodded in agreement. "Yes, yes," they said, "the rebbe's right!"

The Polish thief, the troublemaker, now changed his tune. He too began to weep and said, "Rebbe, I know that you're right. I'm so envious of you Jews that even at a time like this, sitting in prison, you can chant your prayers and sing your songs. You don't give in to the Nazis. Tell me," he said, "what are you praying?"

"This is our holiday of Passover," the rebbe replied. "We're celebrating that long ago, God saved us from the slavery of the Egyptians."

The Pole turned to his friends and said, "Look at how these Jews hold on to their dignity even at a time like this, even when they're persecuted and sitting here in prison. We should imitate them!" Then the Poles said, "Rebbe, can you translate what you're saying into Polish so that we can understand?"

The rebbe replied, "What I recited just now was: 'Not once alone has an enemy risen up against us to destroy us. In each generation, they rise against us'—like Hitler, may his name be blotted out!—'but the Holy One, blessed be He, saves us from their hands!'"

The Poles said, "Rebbe, we Poles are also persecuted! Both the Germans and the Russians have oppressed and persecuted us for centuries. We too have suffered and want freedom. We too believe in God! Can we join your holy ceremony?"

"Of course," said the rebbe. "This is for you too. All humans are made in the image of God. All deserve to be free. Only a murderer erases the divine image from his face. Jews!" said the rebbe. "Make room for our *seder* guests. Make room for our Polish brothers to sit with us. We'll say the *Haggadah* together!" So the Jews made room and sat shoulder to shoulder with the Poles.

The rebbe chanted each verse of the *Haggadah* in Hebrew and then in Polish. At one point in the *seder,* he began to sing a Hasidic *niggun* with Polish words that had originally been a drinking song:

> On Sunday we feasted,
> We drank plenty of wine.
> You must know how to be merry,
> But you must know when to quit.
> Let's make merry!
> Let's rejoice!

When Hasidim sang this *niggun,* they elevated its words into holy meanings—about their divine joy in knowing that God was with them.

Now both Poles and Jews joyously sang the *niggun* together, in Polish. They forgot that they were in prison and entered the spiritual world, the kingdom of God, where all are free. They forgot that Poles and Jews were usually not friends. Now they were friends, and they knew that God would save them from their enemies and from their troubles.

As they sang the *niggun* over and over, they lost themselves in joy, and their singing became so loud that the Nazi guard rushed in again. But this time, seeing the Poles and the Jews sitting with their arms around each other's shoulders and singing together, he was taken aback. "What's going on here?" he yelled. But no one heard him. How could they hear him above the singing? They were in another world. They didn't even know he was there. Burning with anger, he took out his pistol and fired at the ceiling, Bam! Bam!

They all became silent. Then, pointing his pistol at one after the other, his face livid with rage, the Nazi screamed at them, "Shut up or I'll kill all of you!"

They were all quiet until he left. Then both Jews and Poles continued the rest of the *seder* in lowered voices, but none of them was any longer depressed or afraid, and none of them was a slave or a prisoner. Together they joyously sang Passover melodies in whispered tones, and their songs rose straight up to the Heavenly Throne.[2] ◈

Dancing with Your Archenemy

The Talmud tells a famous story to explain why the Second Temple was destroyed.

◈ A wealthy man made a wedding for his son and invited many guests. Due to a mistake, an invitation was delivered to a man he hated and considered his enemy, Bar Kamtza, instead of to his friend Kamtza.

At the wedding feast, the host was surprised to see his archenemy present. He went over to him and said, "Leave!"

The embarrassed guest said, "Please, don't humiliate me in front of everybody. Let me stay and I'll pay for my own food."

The host insisted, "Leave immediately. You can't stay here!"

The guest pleaded, "Please, let me stay. I'll pay for half of the feast!"

But the host was enraged and would not listen. He said, "Get out this minute!"

"I'll pay for the whole wedding," begged the guest. "Don't embarrass me by kicking me out!"

But the host refused to listen and had him thrown out bodily. The ejected guest was furious not only at the host but at the many rabbis present who remained silent and did not protest or intervene on his behalf. He went and slandered the Jews to their Roman rulers, saying that they were rebelling.

The Romans then destroyed Jerusalem and the Temple.[3] ❧

Rabbi Shlomo Carlebach said in the name of Rebbe Nachman of Bratzlav that this wealthy man was not at his own son's wedding. Because if he was, how could he be so filled with hate as to kick out anyone, even his worst enemy? When you are truly joyful, you love the whole world.

❧ Imagine, said Shlomo: You are at your daughter's wedding feast. You are dancing on the table in joy and ecstasy. It is the happiest moment in your life; you are in paradise. Suddenly, you see your archenemy—who was invited by mistake—in the hall. What would you do? You would jump off the table, run over to him, embrace him, and say, "My dear friend, why weren't you at the wedding ceremony, at the *huppah* [bridal canopy]?"—and you would mean it! If you are really at your own daughter's wedding and full of joy, could you still have any hate left in your heart? At that moment, you would love even your worst enemy.[4] ≈◎≈

Rebbe Nachman said that people hate only when they are sad, not when they are joyful. Shlomo's path to achieving peace in the world was not by sitting down and reconciling or negotiating but by transcending in joy, by reaching a level of mystic joy and dancing with your enemies—because it is clear to you that you have no enemies. Shlomo said, "There is only one antidote to hatred: joy. If we are dreaming of the whole world being one, it will only happen with joy."

Portraits in the Ecstasy of Joy

imply knowing that there are mystics who have reached the heights of ecstatic joy can inspire a person. In light of the difficulty of cleaving to God in total devotion, the Talmud teaches that people should cleave to the tzaddikim who cleave to God. A person may not merit to see God face to face, but he can at least see the Divine Presence reflected on the glowing face of a holy man or woman whose inner gaze is ever turned to God.

Some mystics are so brimming with joy that it makes others happy. One cannot come close to such a person without being very happy. Even today, there are Jews who radiate divine joy. Just as nearness to God produces profound peace and joy, so does nearness to a holy person produce peace and joy.

Even stories about the joy of holy people can make a person joyful. Holy people are a proof of the happiness of a life lived in the presence of God. To read or hear it said that closeness to God brings joy is one thing, but to see, even in a story, a saint's joy, ecstasy, and bliss is much more powerful and convincing. We can vividly see the goal before us. "Yes," we say to ourselves, "I want that. I want to be like that. I want mystic joy."

Rebbe Levi Yitzhak of Berditchev

Rebbe Levi Yitzhak of Berditchev was on fire with the love of God that burned in his bones. Among the early rebbes, he was famous for his ecstatic devotion and for the fervor with which he performed the *mitzvot.*

 Tefillin are phylacteries, little leather boxes containing scriptural verses handwritten on parchment that men wear strapped to their head and arm while reciting the morning prayers. According to the Hasidic rebbes, *tefillin* symbolize *d'vekut,* God-consciousness, being attached to God in a tight bond of passionate love. But *tefillin* are not worn during a holiday.

⋙ The night after a holiday, Rebbe Levi Yitzhak could not sleep. He had such longing to put on *tefillin* the next morning that he would remain awake the whole night in expectation, anxiously awaiting the break of dawn when he could don the holy *tefillin.*

 The first night of Sukkot he also stayed awake the whole night waiting for the moment when the first light would arrive so that he could fulfill the *mitzvah* of the Four Species—*etrog, lulav, hadasim,* and *aravot* [citron, palm, myrtle, and willows]—ritually waved on the holiday. When the time came and he ran to take his *etrog* and *lulav* in his hands, his joy knew no bounds, as if he had just found the greatest treasure. He kissed them with all his heart, with the greatest love. And he recited the traditional blessing on them with great joy, with such fervor and *d'vekut* that he was close to expiring.

 That was his way with all objects used for *mitzvot*—to kiss them with all his heart. When he did any *mitzvah,* all his limbs were on fire, in the most wondrous and awesome *d'vekut,* so that he was entirely separated from this world.¹

Once, at dawn on the first day of Sukkot, he ran to get his *etrog,* which was kept in a box in a glass-fronted bureau. In his trance of devotion, he stuck out his hand to grab the *etrog,* broke the glass, and cut his hand. But he did not even feel it! He took the *etrog* and ran to do the *mitzvah!*²

When he sat at the *seder* table on Passover, he would get so excited when one holds up the matzah and says, "This matzah . . ." that he would fall down and roll on the floor under the table in ecstasy. The table would overturn, with all the *seder* plates and matzahs and everything on it. By the time he came to himself, they would have another table all prepared, with matzahs and wine cups, and they would have another clean white *kittel* [robe] for him to wear. And he would say again, "This matzah . . ." like someone who was enlivening himself with something, and he would say, "Ah, ah, this matzah!"

Once, he went to the well to do the *mitzvah* of drawing water for the making of the matzahs and his *d'vekut* was so great that he fell into the well. Fortunately, the water was not deep, so there was no disaster.

When he made the blessing before the reading of the Scroll of Esther on Purim, he would dance right on the top of the stand and almost on the *Megillah* scroll itself.³

THE STAINED TALLIS

＊ Rebbe Levi Yitzhak of Berditchev and Rebbe
Baruch of Medzibuz were both rebbes but were exact
opposites. Rebbe Levi Yitzhak was so fiery, he could not
control himself in his devotion. Rebbe Baruch was con-
trolled and precise in every way; everything was done at
the right time, in the right order. Rebbe Levi Yitzhak
was the utmost in love of God; Rebbe Baruch was the
utmost in fear and awe of God. Both are true paths;
both are holy. When Rebbe Levi Yitzhak would *davven*
(pray), he would begin on one side of the room and end
up on the other side; he would be jumping and leaping,
dancing and rolling on the ground. When he made *kiddush* over the wine on Shabbat, everyone nearby had to
wear raincoats, because he would start to throw himself around, he would raise the cup up, move it down,
this way or that way, and the wine might fly out at any
moment. Rebbe Baruch, by contrast, was quiet and
full of awe in his worship. When he prayed, you could
hardly see his lips moving; he was standing in utter
awe before the King of Kings. While the Berditchever
would get so excited he might throw himself under the
Shabbat table and roll around on the floor in the midst
of the meal, Rebbe Baruch would hardly speak at his
Shabbat table, there would be no singing, and everyone
would sit in absolute awe of the Divine Presence. Rebbe
Baruch was like a prince, regal in all his ways.

Once, Rebbe Levi Yitzhak sent a message to Rebbe
Baruch, asking if he might visit. Rebbe Levi Yitzhak

wanted to have the honor of meeting Rebbe Baruch, who was the grandson of the holy Baal Shem Tov. Rebbe Baruch sent back a message refusing. He said, "Your way and mine are totally opposite. You'll disrupt everything I do here." Rebbe Levi Yitzhak sent another message promising to control himself the whole time he was in Medzibuz. "I'll do everything your way. I won't lead any *davvening* or make *kiddush* at the table on my own; I'll just say 'amen' when you make the blessing over the wine. Because once I get started, I can't control myself. I promise I'll be quiet." So Rebbe Baruch agreed to a visit.

The Berditchever arrived, and Friday night, the Hasidim of Rebbe Baruch were waiting to see the wild devotion in praying that they had heard about. But nothing happened. Rebbe Levi Yitzhak was quiet and well behaved. The Hasidim were surprised. They were waiting to hear his amazing *kiddush*, but he did not even make his own *kiddush* at the Sabbath table; he only said 'amen' quietly when Rebbe Baruch made the blessing over the wine.

Then came the meal. The first course is traditionally fish. There is a Hasidic custom to serve two kinds of fish—sweet fish, like gefilte fish, and sour fish, like herring. It is an issue among the kabbalists and rebbes which to eat first. It is a mystical matter. Should one eat the sweet fish first, to fortify oneself to be able to bear the sour afterward? Or should one eat the sour fish to get that out of the way to have the reward of the sweet later? These represent two ways to live. Both are holy, both are pure, just like the two ways of the Berditchever and the Medzibuzer—love of God and fear of God.

So Rebbe Baruch had a Hasid who went around as a waiter, asking everyone which kind of fish they wanted first. He asked the Berditchever, "Holy Rebbe, which kind of fish do you like?" That is all he had to say. The Berditchever yelled, "Which kind of fish do I like? I don't love fish. I love only God!" With that, he lost it; he grabbed hold of the tray with the fish and threw it up in the air. Pieces of gefilte fish and herring went flying about, and everyone was ducking and taking cover.

But a big piece of fish fell—plop!—right on the beautiful *tallis* [prayer shawl] of Rebbe Baruch, who was sitting at the head of the table. He was in a trance of awe and hardly knew what was happening around him. But the fish landed on his *tallis* and woke him up.

Many of the big rebbes ate the Friday night meal with a prayer shawl on. Usually a *tallis* is not worn at night or when eating. But they put it on while it was still day, prayed with it, and then ate with it on, because their eating was devotional, just like their praying. When the Hasidim saw the big blob of fish dripping on the beautiful *tallis* of their rebbe, they were aghast and ran to wipe it off, but Rebbe Baruch would not let them, because, he said, the stains were holy. He said, "These stains were caused by a Jew who loves only God. How can I wipe them off?" So he never cleaned that *tallis*.

After Rebbe Baruch's death, that *tallis* was considered so precious and holy that it was handed down as an inheritance from one rebbe to another. They wore it

only on Shabbat. During the last century, they wore
it only on Yom Kippur. The last rebbe to possess it was
the Munkatcher Rebbe, who wore that *tallis* only
for the final and holiest service of Yom Kippur, *Ne'ilah.*
The Munkatcher must have known the destruction that
would befall the Jewish people with the Holocaust, because he removed that holy *tallis* from the world and
asked to be buried in it, saying he wanted to be buried
in a *tallis* that had on it stains that were caused by a
Jew who loved only God.[4] ❧

> *D'vekut* is an awareness full of bliss and ecstasy. When peo-
ple are in this blissful state of God-consciousness, like Rebbe Levi
Yitzhak of Berditchev, they can seem as if they are drunk or even insane. In a letter defending Rebbe Levi Yitzhak from those who did
not understand his sometimes strange ways—ecstatically running
around or dancing wildly on the table or falling and rolling on the
floor—Rabbi Eleazar, the son of Rebbe Elimelech of Lizensk, wrote,
"When a tzaddik serves God from fear and from love, that love can
bring him to what almost seems like madness, as it is written, 'In
her love you will always be ravished,'[5] and err as if insane. This is
what we find with King David, when he led the procession bringing
the Ark [with the tablets of the Ten Commandments] up to Jerusalem, 'And David danced and leaped with all his might.'"[6]

Rebbe Shlomo of Zevill

Rebbe Shlomo of Zevill was a great Hasidic rebbe of the previous
generation. There is a photograph of him on the cover of his Hebrew
biography, *Tzaddik Yesod Olam* (A Tzaddik Who Is the Foundation
of the World). The moment you look at this photo of his holy face,
you become his disciple.

Rebbe Shlomo, who was a great rebbe in Zevill, Russia, went, in the middle of his life, to live in Israel and chose to become anonymous. Eight years later, someone who was visiting Israel from the Zevill area recognized him and told everyone, "This is the famous Zeviller Rebbe!" From then on, many people came to him, and he was once again a big rebbe. A few anecdotes tell of the Zeviller Rebbe's mystic joy.

ECSTASY FROM TEFILLIN

According to the Hasidic rebbes, *tefillin* symbolize and induce *d'vekut,* God-consciousness, and *d'vekut* produces bliss. Since *tefillin* are holy objects and a person is supposed to be in an elevated state of consciousness while wearing them, there are certain restrictions relating to their use—for example, that one may not sleep while wearing *tefillin.*

⟨⟩ The Zeviller Rebbe was attached to God every minute of the day—heart and soul—and experienced ecstasy from his *d'vekut.* His ecstasy deepened when he donned *tefillin.* When he was living in Jerusalem anonymously, the Zeviller used to pray in a certain synagogue where no one knew who he was; that is, they did not know that he was anyone special or that he had once been a famous rebbe. But when he said the *Sh'ma,* the "Hear O Israel" prayer, during the morning prayer service, he always went into an ecstatic trance. He would nod out.

Once, someone noticed him and said, "Hey! You're not allowed to sleep in *tefillin!*"[7] ⟨⟩

Occasionally, Hasidic tales, such as this one, tell of simple people and even some sophisticated spiritual people who did not realize that a rebbe had entered a trance of *d'vekut* and instead thought that he had fallen asleep or fainted.

⊰⊱ The Zeviller Rebbe once told his Hasidim that he
"knew someone" in Jerusalem who got more pleasure
from putting on *tefillin* than the most lascivious person
got from lewd behavior. The Hasidim later realized that
the rebbe was talking about himself.[8] ⊰⊱

THE REBBE'S HOLY DANCING

⊰⊱ The Zeviller Rebbe's holy dancing at family weddings was famous, for he danced ecstatically, with great
joy and cleaving to God. Sometimes, after one round of
dancing, he would enter a trance and fall to the ground
in a "faint."[9]

Whenever the rebbe danced at some holy celebration, the whole town of Zevill came to watch. And people
wept from joy as they watched him. His biography says
that they did not know why they were weeping. . . .[10] ⊰⊱

Why were they weeping? Because their dream had come true.
Watching someone like the Zeviller Rebbe rejoice, seeing his holy
ecstatic dancing, they realized that there surely is a God. So they
wept for joy.

Rabbi Yaakov Filmer

⊰⊱ Rabbi Yaakov Filmer was a saintly figure in Jerusalem in the previous generation, a Breslover[11] Hasid
who had grown up in Berditchev in the Ukraine. When
he was a boy, his longing for his Heavenly Father and
for a way to serve Him was so intense that at times

tears would stream from his eyes nonstop. He began to search for a way to serve God and traveled from town to town. He was so restless for God that he was climbing walls.

Once, when he was wandering around the markets and streets of Lemberg seeking his soul's Beloved, his seeming shiftiness attracted the attention of undercover police, who arrested him. When they discovered their mistake, they released him.

In the Song of Songs, the female lover says, "On my bed during the nights, I sought my soul's beloved. I sought him but I found him not. Oh, I must rise now and go about the city, in the marketplaces and streets. I will seek him whom my soul loves. I sought him but I found him not. Then the watchmen who patrol the city streets found me. I asked them, 'Have you found the one whom my soul loves?'"[12] Rabbi Yaakov Filmer was madly restless for God, and what had happened once to the lover of the Song of Songs happened to him.

When Rabbi Yaakov Filmer dwelt in Berditchev, he lived next to the cemetery where Rebbe Levi Yitzhak of Berditchev was buried. More than any other rebbe, Rebbe Levi Yitzhak was mad with love for God. The young Yaakov Filmer used to spend night after night at the Berditchever's holy grave reciting the Midnight Lamentation Service, pleading for the redemption of the Jewish people and the redemption of his own soul from worldliness. He was even given a key to the Berditchever's mausoleum, which he took with him when he later traveled to Jerusalem.

How did he come to travel to Israel and Jerusalem? One Sabbath in Berditchev, when Rabbi Yaakov was thirty-three years old, and they read in the synagogue the Torah verse with God's words to Abraham, "Leave your land, your birthplace, and your father's house . . . ,"[13] he became so filled with longing that he traveled to the Holy Land.

Most of the pious Jerusalemites then were desperately poor and—says the book from which this story comes—their poverty benefited them because it so utterly removed them from this world's vanities and led them to eternal life. But Rabbi Yaakov Filmer was *so* poor and yet *so* happy; it was a wonder! At first glance, he seemed like an ordinary person, but when one looked beyond his ever-smiling face, his frequent jokes, and the Hasidic melodies he always sang, what showed through was the Hasid within, for whom this world's pleasures and troubles together were worth no more than the skin of a garlic.

One well-known rabbi of the time, a prominent Breslover Hasid, said that Rabbi Yaakov's radiant face was clear evidence that he was a hidden tzaddik—his outward simplicity concealing an inner holiness. Another prominent Breslover told that Rabbi Yaakov—who was a tailor by trade—used to repeat aloud memorized teachings from the Kabbalah as he worked on his sewing machine. He said that Rabbi Yaakov once joked to him, "My sewing machine talks Kabbalah."

Rabbi Yaakov used to walk around looking like a beggar, but his alert eyes sparkled, his cheeks were

flushed red from an excess of vitality, and he sometimes complained about the crowds on the streets of
Jerusalem—that people were not happy enough![14] ✥

Rabbi Yaakov Filmer's "complaint" is illuminated by a related
anecdote.

✥ Rabbi Hersh Weissfish, a contemporary of Rabbi
Yaakov Filmer's in Jerusalem, is described as a "happy
Jew." It is said that if you saw him approaching on the
street, you had to smile. If not, when he reached you, he
would say, "*Reb Yid,* my dear fellow Jew, I can see from
your face that you're not so satisfied with the world God
has created." Then Rabbi Hersh would enter into a long
discussion, sometimes for hours, to prove to the person
by many arguments that he should be happy![15] ✥

IT'S GOOD!

Traditional Jews sometimes form a fellowship group called a *havurah*. Friends and comrades join together to pursue some specific type
of good deed, such as gathering regularly to recite psalms or to visit
the sick. Typically, the group has a name, such as the Visiting the Sick
Havurah, and a few rules that are written up in a charter. Members
sign the charter and obligate themselves to follow the rules.

✥ When Rabbi Netta Tzainvirt, a Boyaner Hasid of the
previous generation, saw one of his acquaintances in a
sad mood, with his nose down, Rabbi Netta would speak
to him heart to heart and try to console him and cheer
him up. The rabbi would always repeat that "if a person
knew how great a good had been done for him merely by

his descending to this world, despite everything, he would regret every moment of sadness in his life."

"A Jew knows that everything's good," he would say. "My children are the best for me, my house is the best for me, my life is full of goodness, and everything is good. That's why I'm happy in my world. When a person is joyful, he can accomplish anything, and when he is sad, he can accomplish nothing. Therefore," he would say about himself with a smile, "we called an assembly, sat down, and decided: We have to be joyful!"

Purim, one of the most joyous of Jewish holidays, is about the kind of joy that releases wild and exuberant behavior. On Purim, it is a *mitzvah,* a religious obligation, to drink until drunkenness.

One Purim at the Boyaner synagogue, Rabbi Netta jumped up on a table and boomed out loudly from the depths of his holy inebriation, "I want to start a new *havurah* that will bear the name 'It's Good!' Our fellowship's single rule will be this: To see that everything is good. And if it seems to someone that something is 'not good,' God forbid, the whole *havurah* will yell out three times, 'It's good! It's good! It's good!' Then everything will already be made good for him."[16] ✍

Rabbi Yaakov Arye
of Radzimin

In his later years, Rabbi Yaakov Arye became a Hasidic rebbe in Radzimin. The following three tales are from his youth, when he was extremely poor.

THOU SHALT NOT STEAL

⫷ When Rabbi Yaakov Arye became the rabbi in his hometown of Ritchvil, his weekly rabbi's salary was a pittance, not enough to live on. The community was small and poor and could not afford to pay a rabbi more. So Rabbi Yaakov Arye lived in poverty, and his *rebbetzin*, Hayya, had to supplement his meager income by traveling to the nearby villages to sell pots and pans and in return receive potatoes and vegetables to feed her family—her husband and their children.

Despite his poverty, Rabbi Yaakov Arye was always joyful. He was happy with his portion in life and was satisfied with the little he had. Because of his lack of money, he could not even afford to buy a yarmulke [skullcap] and, like the poorest of the poor Jewish peasants, had to cover his head with a cabbage leaf!

But he would walk around town with a cabbage leaf on his head, with an erect posture, and he radiated joy.

Once, one of the townspeople asked him, "Rabbi, aren't you ashamed of your poverty?"

"Why should I be ashamed of it?" he replied. "Did I steal it from anyone?"[17] ⫸

At first, the rabbi's pointed response seems humorous. But if one considers his words, one realizes that they are not a joke. When you laugh at a holy tale, you should ponder why you are laughing, for it is often because the viewpoint of the holy person in the tale is topsy-turvy compared to that of ordinary people. Why? Because in the viewpoint of a holy person, God, not the ego, is truly at the center. That is what seems funny at first but is deep when considered a second time.

People who are unspiritual, and even many people who are spiritual, expect a poor person to be ashamed of his poverty. Most of us expect a poor person wearing shabby clothes to be embarrassed, but perhaps we should rather expect rich people wearing expensive suits to be embarrassed, for is it possible to become wealthy without stealing in one way or another? It is possible, but it is so difficult and very rare! A person has to be almost holy to engage in business without violating ethical laws.

Rabbi Yaakov Arye was poor, but he was a holy person who stole from no one. And as is true of the most pious people, he rejoiced in his portion, in what God gave him. So he walked around wearing his cabbage-leaf yarmulke and radiated his joy in life.

AN UNFORGETTABLE DANCE

Accepting poverty or any other suffering required to pursue a spiritual path does not make a person miserable and depressed but joyful and exalted.

◈ When Rabbi Yaakov Arye was a young man and a disciple of Rebbe Simha Bunim of Pshis'cha, he befriended another disciple of his master, perhaps the greatest among them, and the one who succeeded him as rebbe—the fiery Rabbi Menahem Mendel of Kotzk.

Once, the two friends—Rabbi Yaakov Arye and Rabbi Menahem Mendel—traveled together to Pshis'cha to be with Rebbe Simha Bunim for the winter holiday of Hanukkah. After Hanukkah, they decided to stay in Pshis'cha with the rebbe for the whole winter. They had no money to support themselves, but each one had a warm sheepskin coat. Rabbi Menahem Mendel's coat was worth eight gold coins, and Rabbi Yaakov Arye's was worth four. So they decided to sell Rabbi Menahem Mendel's coat for the eight gold coins, and they used that money to support themselves for the whole winter. They took turns wearing Rabbi Yaakov Arye's coat. When one of them had to go outside, he used the coat; when the other one needed it, he used it.

After Passover, which is in the spring, they decided to stay in Pshis'cha with the rebbe for the whole summer and until after the Days of Awe—Rosh HaShanah and Yom Kippur—and the other holidays that follow in the early fall. So now they sold Rabbi Yaakov Arye's sheep-skin coat, since in the milder weather they had less need for a warm, heavy coat, and they used the smaller sum they received for his coat to support themselves for the whole summer and beyond.

On the final fall holiday, Simhat Torah, after the conclusion of Rebbe Simha Bunim's holiday feast, Rabbi Yaakov Arye and Rabbi Menahem Mendel danced for four hours straight, and Rabbi Yaakov Arye never forgot that dance. He used to tell how he danced on the table with the holy Rabbi of Kotzk, and that they danced on the table, then came down, then they danced on the table again, up and down, without letup or tiring.[18] ☙

Dancing on a table from an excess of joy symbolizes transcending one's mundane awareness. It also signifies going beyond one's normal limitations, so that what is usually a table for eating can become a platform for dancing. Perhaps their going up and down on the table indicates that although life always has its ups and downs, one can still dance, regardless.

Because these two young men were willing to sacrifice their possessions and comforts, they were able to stay with their rebbe for a whole year. They did not become depressed at giving up even their coats; they finally celebrated their achievement with ecstatic joy, for by their self-sacrifice, they had attained something that is beyond all material value—spiritual freedom and the company of their rebbe and of God.

THE HIDDEN LIGHT

⫷ On another trip that Rabbi Yaakov Arye of Radzimin and Rabbi Menahem Mendel of Kotzk made to their master, Rebbe Simha Bunim, they were forced to stay for Shabbat in a village two miles from Pshis'cha when they saw that they would not be able to reach Pshis'cha before the onset of Shabbat. Since there were no Jews in that village, they had to ask one of the gentiles for hospitality. The man did not invite them into his house but told them they could use his barn.

He did not give them a candle to light for Shabbat, so they had to sit in darkness, which caused them a good deal of anguish. Yaakov Arye said to Menahem Mendel, "Do you see, my friend, that we have no choice but to make use of the light that was hidden since the six days of creation?" [The Book of Genesis says that light was created on the first day but the sun only on the fourth day. The ancient rabbis said that this was the Spiritual Light that God hid to be used by holy people.]

So they stood up in the dark and prayed the Sabbath-welcoming service and evening service and then, since they had no wine, they recited *kiddush* on the bread left over from their journey. After finishing their meal of bread, they sat and shared Torah teachings, sang Sabbath hymns, and danced. The next day, they did the same. They prayed and fulfilled the requirement to eat the two other Sabbath meals by eating the dry bread that remained, and they were joyful–singing, dancing, and sharing Torah teachings the whole day. In this way, they passed the Sabbath.

Immediately after the Sabbath, they harnessed their horse to the wagon and set out for Pshis'cha. But before they arrived, Rebbe Bunim sensed their coming from afar by means of the holy spirit and set out in his carriage to receive them.

When Rabbi Yaakov Arye saw that his holy rebbe was coming toward them, as the vehicles approached, he jumped from his wagon right into the rebbe's carriage, and as he did so, his shoes fell off, but he was so excited that he did not notice.

Only later, when the rebbe asked him, "Where are your shoes? Why are you walking around in socks?" did he realize that his shoes had fallen off when he jumped. He said, "Rebbe, I didn't notice." Then Rebbe Bunim blessed him that he would never have pains in his feet.[19] ⟨⟩

When Rabbi Yaakov Arye jumped out of his shoes with intense joy, he jumped out of the external, physical world to enter the spiritual world. Because of this, the rebbe blessed him with an even deeper spiritual level: that he not feel bodily pain and suffering.

By caring so little about possessions and comforts, Rabbi Yaakov Arye revealed the light of his soul; that is why he could wear shabby clothes and a cabbage yarmulke, yet radiate inner joy; that is why he could dance in a dark barn with the Hidden Light or dance on a table or jump out of his shoes in his joy at being with his rebbe.

Rebbe Shalom Noah of Slonim-Jerusalem wrote that a holy person who abandons bodily desires that separate him from God will experience God's nearness in all the situations and circumstances of life—for "when I dwell in darkness, God is my light," "when I walk in the valley of the shadow of death, I will fear no evil, for You are with me."[20]

Flashes of Godliness

꒜ Rabbi Shmuel, the fourth Rebbe of Lubavitch, told the following tale at his festive table on Shavuot, the Festival of Weeks [celebrating the giving of the Torah on Mount Sinai] in 1881, after saying that "Heaven pays well for sincerity."

"In the days of the first Lubavitcher Rebbe, Rebbe Shneur Zalman of Liadi, there was a Lubavitcher Hasid named Reb Yekutiel from Liyepli, who was, at first, a simple man. But after hearing a Torah teaching from the rebbe about the two metaphorical 'chambers' of the heart—the right chamber, which inclines a person to good, and the left chamber, which inclines him the other way—Reb Yekutiel was so profoundly affected by the rebbe's words that he climbed up to the window of the second-story room in which the rebbe was sitting studying Torah[21]—it was very difficult to get in to see the rebbe—and cried out, 'Rebbe, cut out my left side. I can't do it!'

"The rebbe answered him, 'It's written: "You [God] enliven them all."'

"These few words struck Reb Yekutiel like a lightning bolt from heaven and infused him with spiritual power. From then on, even when he was walking on the street, he occasionally had 'flashes' where he would suddenly see the divinity of all reality and would begin to dance ecstatically. He would walk along and call out in Russian, 'The Hasid is coming!' He was so happy that now he had become a real Hasid."

Rebbe Shmuel said that another Lubavitcher Hasid of that time, who lived in Borisov, used to tell that Reb Yekutiel once came to Borisov and entered the post office to take care of some business, when he had a "flash," whereupon he grabbed the hands of the postal clerk and began to dance with him in the post office!

Rebbe Shmuel concluded his story about Reb Yekutiel by repeating, "Heaven pays well for sincerity. How does it pay? It pays," he said, "with spiritual levels and with divine revelations."[22] ≪◈≫

A great tzaddik can impart spiritual power and divine revelations by a touch, a glance, or a word, as happened with Reb Yekutiel. But a person must be worthy of receiving such a gift.

What did Rebbe Shneur Zalman mean by the verse "You enliven them all"?[23] The Jewish mystics say that this verse means that God enlivens and gives existence and vitality to every creature and creation. Nothing would exist for a single moment were it not for the constant flow of divine will that brings each thing into being and keeps it in existence. When a person sees the spiritual essence of every thing and that its existence emanates from God's Being, he has mystic vision: the world is alive with divinity.

The rebbe also meant that God can enliven all His people, even a simple person like Reb Yekutiel, and give to him this awesome vision.[24] The rebbe removed Yekutiel's "left side," which screens the truth, and "flashed" into him the divine vision, to see divinity in the same way a person sees the material things of the world.

This tale shows that even a simple person who is not a great Torah scholar can have such "flashes," such visions of divinity and divine light, although it says that Reb Yekutiel was only "at first" a simple man, not later. The more devout a person becomes and the more he restlessly seeks God, the more often he will have such experiences and the longer they will last until he will have not just occasional flashes where he sees God's presence and light but will live in that world of divine light and divine bliss. That is the world in which Reb Yekutiel's rebbe, Rebbe Shneur Zalman, lived.

Although Reb Yekutiel experienced "only" flashes of divinity, even they brought joy and ecstasy. How did Reb Yekutiel attain this? Why was he blessed by the rebbe? Because of his earnestness and sincerity, for with his intense yearning for God, he metaphorically and literally climbed up to the rebbe's level, so to speak, for a brief moment, and cried out for help.[25] And as Rebbe Shmuel explained, Heaven pays well for sincerity. How does it pay? With spiritual levels and revelations. And with mystic joy.

The Effect of Viewing a Holy Face

There is a Hasidic concept of an *atzmi,* a tzaddik of perfect integrity, who lives totally from his soul, his inner being; he is himself in every circumstance. Viewing the face of such a person can be an awesome experience; one is nullified before the light of such a soul.

Rebbe Avraham Matityahu of Shtepinesht was a son of the Rizhiner Rebbe. Whoever looked at the holy face of the Rebbe of Shtepinesht had his heart stirred to repentance, sometimes becoming a completely different person.

There was a certain very wealthy Jew named Hersh Wexler, who lived in the town of Jassy in Romania. Unfortunately, this Reb Hersh had drifted very far from the Jewish religion. But he owned large farms and vineyards and other properties near Shtepinesht and from time to time visited there to supervise his extensive enterprises.

Once, when he was in the vicinity of Shtepinesht on the holy Sabbath and was galloping along on his horse accompanied by mounted aides (it is forbidden to ride a horse or to engage in business activities on the Sabbath), he passed by the courtyard of the holy rebbe's residence. This was in the morning, when the rebbe always stood for a few minutes meditating before prayer, staring out the window of his house. As this Hersh Wexler raced by on his horse, he turned and saw the rebbe's face in the window and was stunned by his awesome and radiant holiness. The rebbe's face expressed compassion, deep wisdom, and a peace beyond anything in this world. His face glowed with the light of the *Shechinah.*

Reb Hersh was so affected by this awe-inspiring sight that he could not contain himself. He pulled his horse to an abrupt stop, jumped off, and giving the reins to one of his aides, ran into the rebbe's house, saying, "I want to repent!"

The rebbe greeted him affectionately, befriended him, and told everyone to treat him in the best way. He told Reb Hersh to begin keeping the Sabbath and the other *mitzvot,* and this Hersh Wexler actually became another person—with a beard and *payot* [sidelocks]— and completely repented. He became one of the rebbe's closest Hasidim. He visited Shtepinesht for all the holidays and would not only dance in ecstasy but arouse all the other Hasidim to fervent dancing.

He kept all the *mitzvot,* the light as well as the heavy, and was so close to the rebbe that on Purim, as part of the fun, he always used to dress up as a doctor and medically examine the rebbe with a stethoscope and such. And he would interview him in German, which the rebbe understood [all the great doctors then were German], saying, "Yes, *Herr Rabbiner,* how are you feeling?" and other questions, to make the rebbe laugh—because the holy rebbe was always very serious—and Reb Hersh succeeded in making him smile and even laugh at his antics.[26] ⬦

The Holy Clock

⬦ When Rebbe Yaakov Yitzhak, the holy Seer of Lublin, died, and the *shiva,* the seven days of intense mourning, had passed, his heirs cast lots and divided up his clothes, his personal effects, and various other objects that he had used during his life. The Seer's son, Rabbi Yosef of Turchin, inherited his father's white silk Sabbath garments and an old clock that was in his holy father's room and by whose chimes the Seer regulated the hours of his divine service—so much time for studying Torah, so much time for prayer, and so on.

Rabbi Yosef folded the clothes to make a package for the clock, to keep it from being broken. Then he put the package in his knapsack, swung it over his shoulder, and started out for home with his attendant. Being poor, he went on foot. While they were on the road, a drizzle started to fall, followed quickly by increasing rain until it was pouring. After a quarter of an hour, the downpour was so great that he could not continue traveling and he had to seek shelter. By the time he reached a village, he was drenched, and his clothes were soaking wet. He went into a Jewish inn to stay for a few hours and rest. When the rain let up, he would continue on his way. He waited for an hour, then two, but the rain kept coming down. It poured the whole night, with sporadic thunder and lightning.

He got up in the morning, prayed the morning prayer service, and ate breakfast, but the rain had not stopped. The skies opened and were pouring down torrential rains. No one was entering or leaving the village, and he was forced to stay there. He remained in the inn, eating and then sleeping there that night, both he and his attendant.

The next day, when the rain finally stopped and the skies cleared, he got ready to leave, and the innkeeper brought him the bill for his expenses. Rabbi Yosef took out his wallet and looked into it but found only enough money to pay for one day. "I want to pay everything I owe you," he said to the innkeeper, "but I'm embarrassed to say that it seems I don't have enough money with me. But I do have some articles that are worth something, some holy personal effects that I inherited from my father, may he rest in peace. They're right here. Take a look at them, and maybe you can find something that appeals to you,

to take for what I owe you." As he spoke, he took the
package out of his knapsack, untied it, and showed
the innkeeper the silk clothes and the old clock. He did
not tell the innkeeper who he was and that his father was
the famous Seer of Lublin; undoubtedly, it pained Rabbi
Yosef to have to give anything away from the precious legacy of his father's personal effects, but what could he do?

The innkeeper looked the things over, turned
them this way and that, to see what they were and to
get an idea of what they were worth, but he did not
know what to say. So he called his wife over, told her the
story—that the guest did not have enough money and
wanted to pay with these items—and said, "Let's take
them into the other room where we can talk privately
and decide if they have any value to us and if we should
take them." The woman carefully gathered the things
together, tied them up again, and took them into the
other room, her husband following after her.

They spread the clothes out on the table, and the
woman began to feel them, to see what they were made
of and judge their value. She and her husband did not
want to be cheated. She rubbed the silk clothes between
her fingers and said, "These are actually expensive
clothes, real silk, but they are worth nothing to us. Not
many people would be interested in buying them from
us, and you have no use for them: They are holy garments; they are not for a village Jew like you. We'll just
take the clock, if it works." After satisfying herself that
it did work, she said, "It's old, but it's still running, and
we can use it to know the exact time to milk the cow—

morning, afternoon, and evening. We'll be able to milk
her every day at the same time; it will be good for the
cow and good for us."

Her husband agreed. He returned the clothes to the
guest, but they kept the clock, which he hung on the wall
in his bedroom. Rabbi Yosef then left and continued on
his way home. The clock chimed out the exact time,
every hour, and no one paid any further attention to it.

Years later, a great rebbe, Rebbe Dov Ber of Radoshitz, who had been a disciple of the Seer of Lublin,
passed through that town on a journey somewhere.
When he arrived, the sun was setting and he had to stay
there overnight. He went in to the innkeeper and asked
for a separate room so that he could continue his Torah
study and divine service as usual without being disturbed. The innkeeper told him that he did not have any
private rooms; there was just one large common guest
room. But since the innkeeper knew that Rebbe Dov
Ber was a famous rebbe, he offered him his own room
and said he would sleep in the guest room. Seeing that
there was no other choice, the tzaddik accepted his
offer, thanked him, and went into the inner room.

When the innkeeper was preparing for sleep, he
heard the footsteps of the rebbe pacing about in the adjacent room, singing and then dancing. He waited for a
while and fixed his bed, thinking, "In a little while, he'll
stop dancing and singing and go to sleep." But when
the innkeeper was in bed, tired from his hard day of
work and drifting in and out of sleep, his guest was still
joyfully singing and dancing, and the innkeeper could

not fall asleep. He was turning in his bed the whole night. He became very angry but did not go in to his guest or complain because after all, this was a great rebbe! What could he say to him?

Shortly before dawn, the innkeeper finally fell asleep, and when he awoke, it was already broad daylight. He hurried and got up from his bed. But when he went out of the guest room and saw the rebbe going out from his own room, he remembered what had transpired during the night. He wanted to ask the rebbe why he had been singing and dancing until dawn but did not know how to bring up the subject in the right way. While he was standing there, scratching himself and thinking, the tzaddik came over to him and asked, "Tell me, where did you get that clock in your bedroom?"

The innkeeper was taken aback by the question. Why was the holy Rebbe of Radoshitz interested in his clock? But since he asked, he told him that many years ago, someone had stayed at his inn, eating and sleeping, for two days, and when he did not have enough money to pay his bill, the guest gave him the clock instead.

"You don't know what a treasure that clock is," said the rebbe. "That is the clock of the holy Seer of Lublin. As soon as I entered the room and heard its chimes, I recognized it."

The innkeeper was even more surprised now and asked, "Is there some kind of identification on the clock that you recognized it? And what's different about its chimes? It sounds to me just like any other clock."

"When an ordinary clock chimes," replied the rebbe, "it tells those who hear it that the years of their lives are passing on; one more hour is lost and gone, never to return. Now, even though this information is important, because it spurs people to repent and do good deeds, it is still permeated with gloom and sadness, because it reminds them of the day of their death.

"But the clock of the holy Seer of Lublin, of blessed memory, is different. The holy Seer used this clock for many years to regulate his daily schedule of divine service. So its hourly chimes ring out good news of joy and happiness: 'I'm one hour closer to the goal, one hour closer!' When I heard that chime, how could I sleep? I was so happy that I had to sing and dance the whole night."[27] ⌘

How do we live *our* lives? Is each hour that passes one more hour gone, bringing us closer to death, or are we one hour closer to our spiritual goal of getting close to God?

The holy clock of the Lubliner represents the path of serving God with joy. There is a difference between the sad way of serving God from fear and awe, concentrating on our faults and sins; and the joyful way of serving Him from love, aware of how we are constantly coming closer to Him. If our religious involvement makes us happy, we will make more spiritual progress than if we constantly discourage ourselves and make ourselves miserable because of our failures. Instead of burdening ourselves with guilt and thinking, "I'm not doing this! I'm not accomplishing that!" we should think, "Ah, even this little bit I'm doing is so good, it makes me so happy, I want to do more!" If the clock of our lives chimes that we are constantly getting closer to God, we will always be singing and dancing in joy.

How to Be Joyful

*I*t is valuable to know that Judaism leads to ecstatic joy, but how does one actually attain it? The Jewish mystic path provides rewards of joy that come naturally. But the tradition also provides specific teachings about reaching joy, bliss, and ecstasy. The essence revolves around striving for devotion and fervor; about throwing oneself into the pursuit of what is most important one hundred percent, without reserve; about seeking real spiritual experience; about focusing on love for God and for human beings, who are created in the divine image.

When one strives to see the divine reality behind the veil spread across the world, one will reach the place of joy; when one has no expectations and receives everything as coming from God's own hand, one will taste joy and bliss; when one abandons a false attachment to material possessions, one will know true happiness; when one sings and dances and does whatever one can for the glory of God, one will be filled with the spirit of joy. The stories in this section answer the question, "How can I get there?"

The Baal Shem Tov Learns
Love of God from a Shepherd

⟨⟩ The Baal Shem Tov was once shown from heaven that a certain shepherd named Moshe served God better than he did. He longed to meet this shepherd, so he ordered his horses harnessed to his coach and traveled, with a few of his disciples, to the place where he was told the shepherd lived.

They stopped in a field at the foot of a hill and saw above on the hillside a shepherd who was blowing his horn to call his flock. After the sheep gathered to him, the shepherd led them to a nearby trough to water them. While they were drinking, he looked up to heaven and began to call out in a loud voice, "Master of the world, You are so great! You created heaven and earth and everything else! I'm a simple man, ignorant and unlearned, and don't know how to serve You or to praise You. I was orphaned as a child and raised among gentiles, so I never learned any Torah. But I have a shepherd's horn that I can blow on like a *shofar.*' I'll blow on it with all my strength, to proclaim, 'The Lord is God!'" After blowing with all his might on the horn, he collapsed to the ground, without an ounce of energy, and lay there motionless until his strength returned.

Then he began again and said, "Master of the world, I'm just a simple shepherd; I don't know any Torah, and I don't know how to pray. What can I do for You? The only thing I know is to sing shepherds' songs." He immediately began to sing loudly and fervently with all his strength until, again, he fell to the earth exhausted, without an ounce of energy.

After recovering, he began again and called out, "Master of the world! What is it worth that I blew on my horn and sang songs for You, when You're so great? What more can I do to serve You?" He paused for a moment and said, "There's something else I know how to do, and I'll do it for Your honor and Your glory!" He then stood on his head and began to wave his feet wildly in the air. Then he did somersaults one after the other until he collapsed on the ground exhausted. The Baal Shem Tov and his disciples watched all this from a distance in amazement.

The shepherd lay there silently until his strength returned. Then he began to speak again and said, "Master of the world, I've done what I can, but I know it's not enough! What more can I do to serve You?" After pausing to reflect, he said, "Yesterday, the lord who owns the flock made a feast for his servants, and when it ended, he gave each of us a silver coin as a gift. I'm giving that coin to You as a gift, O God, because You created everything and feed all creatures, including me, Moshe, the humble shepherd!" Saying this, he threw the coin upward.

At that moment, the Baal Shem Tov saw a hand reach out from heaven to receive the coin. He said to his disciples, "This shepherd has taught me how to fulfill the verse: 'And you shall love the Lord your God with all your heart, with all your soul, and with all your might.'"[2] ≈≫

We can add: "with all your joy." Fervent prayer, with love and joy, with all one's energy, to the limits of self-sacrifice, was the path of the Baal Shem Tov too. And it produces revelations of God.

Rebbe Zusya Never Afflicted

⊰⊱ Two disciples of Rebbe Dov Ber, the Maggid of Mezritch, once asked their master, "The Rabbis say that a person should rejoice in his afflictions and bless God for the bad just as he makes a blessing to thank Him for the good. How is that possible?" These disciples were two brothers—Rabbi Shmelke (later of Nikolsburg) and Rabbi Pinhas (later of Frankfurt-on-Main). The Maggid sent them to ask their question to another disciple of his, Rabbi Zusya of Hanipol.

They went to Rabbi Zusya's broken-down cottage and found him smoking his pipe. They told him that the Maggid had sent them to him to ask him their question—"How can one thank and bless God for the bad?"

Like some other holy people, Rabbi Zusya was on a very high spiritual level where he never used the word *I* but instead always referred to himself as "Zusya." He said to them, "Zusya can't understand why the Maggid sent you to him, since Zusya has never experienced anything bad in his whole life!"

Now everyone knew that in fact Rabbi Zusya had suffered greatly in his lifetime: He was poor and sickly. Yet they also knew and saw that he always glowed with inner peace and joy. ⊰⊱

Why was Rabbi Zusya able to joyfully accept poverty and suffering without tasting their bitterness? Because he believed that there was a hidden good in his afflictions—not merely that what was bad would turn into good at a future time but that his afflictions were good now, at the very moment. The pious and mystic view is that afflictions also show God's love for us. They are sent from heaven for our good, to purify our souls, if we react to them by searching out our faults and humbly turning to God. That is why it is a pious custom to refer to the events in one's life not as being "for good or for bad" but to say "for good or to become better."

Rabbi Shneur Zalman of Liadi, the first Lubavitcher Rebbe, told a parable that explains Zusya's attitude: "A king, in all his glory, himself washed the filth from his only son, because of his great love for him."[3]

Zusya knew himself to be a child of God and experienced in his suffering the loving care of his Heavenly Father. He did not feel the "pain of the scrubbing"; instead, he rejoiced in the spiritual benefit he derived from it, for his Father the King was cleaning him of his filth—his sins.

This profound religious teaching about suffering is not an easy lesson for people of our time who are often weak in faith. When someone is beginning to struggle with faith, he first has to work on himself to be certain that he firmly believes that all the good he receives comes from God. Only later can he begin to work on accepting the deeper but more difficult truth that what seems bad is also from God and conceals great good. When a person attains that, he is in a state called "being in the Garden of Eden."

Pious Jews always answer a question about their welfare with "*Baruch HaShem!*"—"Praise God!"—thanking God for whatever comes to them, good or bad. An anecdote about a great Musar teacher, Rabbi Simha Zissel Ziv of Kelm, casts light on the tale about Rabbi Zusya: "When Rabbi Simha Zissel was sick and people asked him how he was, he would sometimes answer, '*Baruch HaShem,* I'm feeling worse today.'"[4]

This seems humorous, but we should ponder its deeper meaning. Were Rabbi Simha Zissel's words of blessing, thanking God for his worsening illness, merely on his lips? Is it possible to thank God for discomfort and sickness? The answer is yes, for God's closeness produces ecstasy. A person may be suffering physically, emotionally, or psychically and, on a deeper level of consciousness, experience his closeness to God as ecstasy. There may be a raging storm on the ocean's surface, but below, in the depths, all is calm and peaceful. Although it may seem contradictory, one can be both miserable and blissful at the same time. When a person lovingly accepts whatever comes from God's hand, he will experience mystic joy and the bliss of God's nearness, always, at every hour and moment, in both good times and bad times.

Rebbe Zusya About Joy and Anger

⪼ The town of Hanipol had a rebbe and a rabbi. Rebbe Zusya was a Hasidic rebbe, and there was a rabbi who ruled on matters of Jewish religious law. Rebbe Zusya did not, however, have a congregation of Hasidim. The Maggid of Mezritch told his son, Rabbi Avraham the Angel, never to try to make Rebbe Zusya a leader of Hasidim because he was above that; he was on a higher level. But people did come to him for help and advice.

Rebbe Zusya, personally, had much trouble all his life, but he was always full of joy. The rabbi, by contrast, was rich and had a good salary, but he was always angry, always bitter. Now, a person who hates other people finally begins to hate himself. One day, the rabbi simply couldn't stand himself anymore. He decided to go to Rebbe Zusya. But he was worried about his prestige and what people would think. So he went at night when nobody would see him. He came to Rebbe Zusya and asked, "Why are you always happy, and why am I always angry?"

He replied, "Zusya will explain it to you. Take the wedding of the rich man's daughter last week. [In those days, one did not send out invitations to a wedding by mail. A rich man had a *gabbai*, a manager, who went from house to house.] The *gabbai* knocked on your door and said, 'Moshe the Rich Man has the honor and pleasure of inviting you to his daughter Feigeleh's wedding on such a date and at such a time.' You said, 'Let me see the list.' You thought, 'I'm number sixteen on the list. What chutzpah! I'm the rabbi of the city! I'm the one performing the wedding! And me, number sixteen! I'm supposed to be number one!' After the manager left, you said, 'I'll show him. I'll come three hours late. They won't be able to start without me. They'll see how important I am!'

"So you came three hours late. Meanwhile, they found someone else to perform the wedding. By the time you arrived, everybody was already sitting down at the table waiting for the meal. Nobody paid any attention to you. Finally, the rich man saw you and said, 'Oh, our rabbi! We waited for you. But we couldn't wait any longer. Please come to the head table.' But the head table was completely filled. So they put your chair behind somebody else. When the waiter brought the food, he didn't see you. So you weren't served. You were so angry! You were cursing the bride and groom; you were cursing God. Finally, the rich man saw that you had nothing to eat. He said, 'Oh, Rabbi, please forgive me. I'm so sorry you didn't get food!' He went into the kitchen and collected some of the leftovers. When he brought it to you, you got even more angry. 'What chutzpah! I'm the rabbi of the city, and they bring me leftovers!' As the wedding feast was coming to an end, you consoled yourself: 'Soon they'll honor me to recite one of the wedding blessings after the Grace.' But by now the rich man had already forgotten that you were there. He called on somebody else. You went home, cursing your wife, cursing your children, cursing the bride, cursing the groom, cursing God. You were angry!"

Zusya continued, "But see what happened with Zusya. The rich man's *gabbai* came to Zusya's door and said, 'Moshe the Rich Man has the honor and pleasure of inviting you to his daughter Feigeleh's wedding at such a time and place.' Zusya said to himself, 'Zusya can't understand it. Zusya's never done anything good to him. Why should Zusya have the privilege to be invited? And if he's such a good friend to Zusya, Zusya wants to be a good friend to him.'

"So Zusya went three hours early, to help them set up everything. When you were late, they asked Zusya to perform the wedding. Zusya sat at the head table. Zusya was asked to recite one of the wedding blessings and the Grace After Meals. Finally, Zusya went home and was loving to his wife and his children.

"So you see, *you expect everything, and whatever you receive is too little, so you're angry. Zusya*

expects nothing, so he's always happy no matter what
*happens."*⁵ ◄◊►

Dancing into Gehinnom

◄◊► When Rebbe Elimelech of Lizensk–Rebbe Zusya's
brother–was a young man, he had a good friend named
Rabbi Shimon who was his study partner; they regularly studied Torah together. Rabbi Shimon was a *gaon*
[a great Torah scholar] but was not involved in Hasidism or piety and did not travel, as his friend Rebbe
Elimelech did, to the Maggid of Mezritch (then head of
the Hasidic movement).

Years later, when Rebbe Elimelech had become
one of the leaders of the Hasidic movement, Rabbi
Shimon encountered his friend surrounded by a group
of Hasidim who were his devoted admirers. Address-
ing him familiarly, without a title of respect such as
"Rabbi," he said to him, "Elimelech, why do the Hasidim
make such a fuss about you? Don't I also know how to
study Torah? Even if you know a little more than me, I
still don't understand why the Hasidim make such a big
to-do about you or what's so special about what you
learned from the Maggid."

Rebbe Elimelech answered his friend, "Shimon,
the difference between us is in only one thing. You
know that a time will come when we'll both have to appear before the Heavenly Court and give an accounting
for our deeds in this world. Now, when they'll ask you

what you did during your life, you'll say, 'Shimon studied Torah; Shimon did *mitzvot.*' They'll immediately begin to investigate your Torah study and *mitzvot* and will undoubtedly find faults and deficiencies—ulterior motives and so on. Then they'll decree that you go to *gehinnom* to be purged. When you hear this verdict, you'll put your hand on your heart and say, 'They'll send Shimon to *gehinnom*? I, Shimon, will go to *gehinnom*?' And you won't want to go, certainly not of your own free will. So they'll have to drag you there against your will. And this struggle of being dragged there will actually be worse than *gehinnom* itself.

"But if they'll ask me, 'What did you do in this world?' I'll tell the truth, because I learned from my rebbe and teacher to tell only the truth. So I'll say to them, 'I know, my masters, that my studying was worth nothing and that the *mitzvot* I did were worthless.'

Immediately, they'll decree that I be sent to *gehinnom.*

"Then I'll ask them, 'What benefit is there from this *gehinnom*? Why does it exist?'

"They'll certainly tell me, '*Gehinnom* is to purify your soul so that you'll be able to appear before the Throne of Glory.' When I hear that, I'll dance into *gehinnom,* and my pleasure and delight from it will be greater than that from the Garden of Eden."[6] ❧

Many tzaddikim, in their humility and with their acute awareness of God's greatness, consider all their divine service and deeds as inadequate. This tale contrasts the attitudes of a pious Hasid and an arrogant Torah scholar. It also helps us understand how some great and holy people are able to accept difficulties and sufferings in this world: They see such afflictions as purifications and rejoice in them. (Compare the parable on page 140 in the name of Rebbe Zusya.) Another anecdote about Rebbe Elimelech makes this matter clearer.

≈≈ After the passing of Rebbe Elimelech of Lizensk, Rebbe Yisrael, the Maggid of Kozhnitz, said with a smile, "When the rebbe appeared before the Heavenly Court, they asked him about his deeds.

"He replied, 'I didn't pray. I didn't study Torah.'

"They decreed, 'If so, let him go to *gehinnom*.' But really they led him to the Garden of Eden.

"When he arrived there, he began to joyously clap his hands, saying, 'If *gehinnom* is this good, how much more so is the Garden of Eden good and beautiful!'– because he thought he was in *gehinnom*."[7] ≈≈

This anecdote clarifies a problem. One may suppose that some tzaddikim who are excessively humble and consider themselves of little worth are depressed and miserable. This story suggests that although "they think they are in *gehinnom*," so to speak, they are really joyful and in the Garden of Eden, *even in this world*.

There is another interesting point. The first anecdote ends with Rebbe Elimelech saying that he will get more joy from dancing into *gehinnom* than from being in the Garden of Eden. This means that for him, doing God's will and being close to God are more dear than any other reward, even the pleasures and delights of paradise.

The second anecdote ends with him saying that if it is so good in *gehinnom*, how much better is it in the Garden of Eden—where he will go once purged by punishment of his sins. This means that Rebbe Elimelech accepted whatever difficult situation God placed him in and only expected greater joy in the future.

The Shirt of a Happy Man

The Rabbis say that the secret of happiness is to be satisfied with your portion, with what God has given to you in this world. Someone who is unsatisfied with his portion and who chases after luxuries and excessive pleasures can never be satisfied; his life is full of bitterness. A teaching story explains this.

↔ A king's son became ill from sadness and depression. The king sought out many doctors, but none of them were able to cure the prince. Then a doctor arrived from a distant land and after examining the boy said that he had found a way to cure him: the prince must wear the shirt of a happy man.

The king sent his servants to wealthy men who lived in big mansions, thinking that they certainly must be happy, but they told the servants that they were not happy because of their many worries and anxieties about their businesses. The king next sent the servants to other wealthy and successful men, traders and builders, but the servants returned with the same answer. Finally, they went to a shepherd, who told them that, yes, he is truly happy. But when they asked him for his shirt, he opened his jacket and showed them that he had no shirt.[8] ↔

Rabbi Yaakov Naiman, a Musar teacher of the previous generation in Israel, taught that true joy can be attained only when a person realizes that the purpose of life is not to be found in possessions or in the externals of this world. Someone who focuses on wealth and success can never reach inner joy; in fact, he usually lacks joy, because joy is something spiritual, and only those who draw close to God can achieve it. All the desires and vanities of this world only depress a person and spiritually diminish him. Someone sunk in worldly vanities is a prey to jealousy and lust, which prevent him from being joyful, because it always seems to him that he lacks something. But if a person realizes that this world is only the outside—the external side of reality—he is jealous of no one and is filled with joy at what he has.[9]

Rebbe Moshe of Kobrin said, "How full this world is of light and sweetness for someone who is not immersed in it. But how dark and bitter the world is for someone who is immersed in it. A person who cleaves to God in *d'vekut* experiences great delight and is unaffected by all the vicissitudes of time and circumstance."[10]

Somersaulting for the Holy Flock of Lambs

⋙ In a small town in Eastern Europe lived a synagogue caretaker named Moshe. On Simhat Torah, Reb Moshe turned into a different person. The pious scholar and elderly man of about seventy was transformed into a mischievous, naughty child and a carefree, happy youth to whom everything was permitted.

At dusk on *Shemini Atzeret* [the eighth-day conclusion of Sukkot that leads into Simhat Torah], he would burst into the synagogue, leaping and cavorting and doing somersaults on the floor. Then he would jump up and cry out to the children in the synagogue, "Holy flock!" and the children, who were waiting for his call, answered by crying out together, like a flock of little lambs, "*Maaaaa!*" This was the signal for Simhat Torah to begin. Reb Moshe would begin it with a special song, whose lyrics went, "We are what we are, but we're still Jews!" and everyone would answer in chorus, "We are what we are!"[11] ⇜

In the first tale in this section, the Baal Shem Tov learned love of God from a shepherd who did somersaults. Some of the early Hasidim, in their ecstatic joy, did somersaults for God during worship. Rebbe Avraham of Kalisk's Hasidim regularly somersaulted and were persecuted for it. Some held the idea that one totally "rolled over" spiritually, reversing up and down for God. Somersaulting also indicates a total disregard for one's dignity and appearance. During worship, one cannot be self-conscious and God-conscious at the same time.

Reb Moshe in this tale obviously enjoyed children. Some holy people spend time with children in order to develop a childlike nature, what the Rabbis call *temimut,* pious innocence. Rebbe Meir Shlomo Yehuda of Mezritch taught, "Why do the Rabbis tell us to bring children and infants to the synagogue and say that there is a reward for doing so? What is the reward?—that we will be able to pray like children, with innocence and simplicity."[12] Part of the secret of achieving ecstasy and joy in worship is to learn to be like a child.

After Reb Moshe's somersaulting and his cry and response to the children, he began Simhat Torah with a song celebrating that although we recognize our faults, we are joyful because in any case we are still Jews!

Somersaulting for the Glory of God

Rebbe Kalonymus Kalman Shapira of Peasetzna, who perished in the Holocaust, once reflected back on a time when he had somersaulted for the glory of God. He wrote:

⇜ If a Jew becomes a new creation, creating within himself the holiness of the People of Israel, then all his actions, even those that are not *mitzvot* or other

prescribed deeds but that he invents for himself to do
at the moment, will make his physical body itself holy;
he will boil, bubble, fizz, and be sanctified.

Why else did I become so aroused when I decided
to make the somersault at the installation of the new
Torah scroll at the synagogue? Why did my very bones
shake when I saw the place where I would dance and
somersault, so that my whole body trembled?

Many times, a Jew's yearning bursts forth from
his spiritual situation or his Torah study or prayer, and
he thinks, "Oh, if only there were some great deed that
I could do for God!" His heart falls within him, and he
thinks, "What are my study or prayer worth after all?
If I'm not satisfied with them, how much less satisfied
must be the One who is the essence of purity and the
source of holiness?" Even when he is not burning to
sacrifice himself in action, he is still longing, "Oh, if
only there were something great I could do, so that even
briefly I could uproot the lowliness of my heart from
my heart, of my body from my body, my self from my
self, and leap toward God!"

When I began to prepare myself for the *siyum*
[celebrating the completion of an extended course of
Torah study] and the installation of the Torah scroll,
a powerful desire burst forth within me, ever-growing,
like a fire in my bones. "Isn't a time like this, of holy and
awesome joy, something that may occur only once in my
whole lifetime? What can I do now physically, actively,
for God? I'll rejoice with awe and trembling, and I'll
dance with all my might. Good, but my soul still won't be

satisfied with that. That is still not the great deed fitting
for an exalted, unique, and holy hour like this."

I thought to myself, "I'll do a somersault, like some
lowly people might do to entertain their master and in
his honor." But the Satan tried to prevent me, saying,
"Why should you do this? What sense is there to it? What
does God, blessed be He, care if you somersault or not?
You might even hurt yourself and damage your health!
Won't doing a somersault in front of everybody make you
contemptible in their eyes, like a fool or a madman?"

Then, from the innermost chamber of my heart,
I moaned and roared, "May God rebuke you, O Satan! It's
not a time to make calculations. It's a critical and unique
moment, a time to perform an act of self-sacrifice for my
Rock and my Creator; that's what I want! And since you've
threatened my health to frighten me and promised to
drench me in mockery and ridicule, now I have the great
deed I sought. Therefore, I've decided to do it and be
sanctified to God!"

From that moment, this lowly and trivial deed that
I thought up became sanctified in my eyes and became
precious to me, and I decided to nullify myself before
it. My body trembled as I began to consider how to perform the somersault, and my soul immediately began to
burn with self-sacrifice. I was no longer thinking only
of a simple act of somersaulting; I now imagined an
altar of God shining before me. . . . The place we would
pass by where the Torah scroll would be installed . . .
became sanctified and seemed to burst out in flames as
my blood began to boil and tears flowed from my eyes.

Why was this hour sanctified because of an act I myself thought up at that moment? Why was my body sanctified and aching to act? It was from the holy sparks that had gathered in my body and were now manifesting, sparks that the least person in Israel merits.[13] And how thrilled I was afterward to see in a commentary to the *Midrash*[14] that says explicitly that King David somersaulted before the holy Ark as he danced with fervor when leading it in procession up to Jerusalem.[15] ➴

Dancing into Jerusalem

➴ Rabbi Shlomo Carlebach said, "We Jews have a dream of going to Jerusalem, but the truth is that only a few of us know the real meaning of going up to Jerusalem. You can see the difference between Jerusalem and other cities when you're in a plane going to Israel and the pilot says, 'We'll be landing in five minutes.' If you're on your way to Paris or London or New York, people yawn, stretch, and say, 'Oh, thank heaven that's over with.' The feeling is one of relief. But if you're on El Al and the pilot says, 'Five minutes to landing,' you get goose bumps.

"Once, I was on an El Al plane to Israel and was reciting the daily prayers in my seat. I closed my eyes and prayed, 'Master of the world, let me see someone on this plane who knows what it is to enter Jerusalem.' I opened my eyes, and sitting opposite me was a beautiful sixteen-year-old girl who, I could tell, knew where she was going.

"Her parents were sitting to her right and left. I said to her, 'Is this your first time going to Jerusalem?' She said, 'Yes!' and she said it not just with the word, but with her eyes, her heart, her whole being. I started to talk to her about the Land of Israel and Jerusalem, and sparks were coming out of her eyes she was so alive. We were talking and laughing together. She introduced me to her parents, but they were so cold and unhappy that the conversation soon ended. When I looked at her parents, they looked sour, like Mr. and Mrs. Sourcream. It seemed it had been a long time since there had been any tenderness between them.

"The whole rest of the flight I was praying, 'Please, God, show me how to help this young woman go up to Jerusalem, because she knows what it means!'

"When we got off the plane, I was able to go through customs more quickly because I have an Israeli passport. And then God made it clear to me what I should do. I went over to a friend of mine who is in charge of all the porters in the Tel Aviv airport, all the luggage carriers. I told him, 'There's a special girl on this flight arriving here for the first time, and I need your help.' So he arranged a little strike of all the luggage carriers, and no luggage was moving. Everyone gathered around the luggage terminal, but no bags were coming out."

Meanwhile, Shlomo's followers from the *moshav*– Ma'or Modi'in, his communal settlement in Israel–were there to greet him and welcome him back to Jerusalem with all their musical instruments. They began to play, and Shlomo said, "We were singing and dancing with

all our hearts while the other people standing around
were watching or joined us. I heard someone saying,
'This could never happen in New York or London, only
Jerusalem!'

"I had closed my eyes, but when I opened them,
I saw the girl from the plane watching what was happening, her eyes wide with joy. When we came to a piece
of the music where I didn't have to sing but the music
went on, I called over one of the young women in our
group and whispered in her ear, 'Go over and bring that
girl into the circle.'

"When I started to sing again, she danced over to
her, grabbed her hand, and led her into the dance. And
the girl began to dance. As I watched, my eyes began to
flow with tears because she reminded me of King David
dancing before the Ark going up in procession to Jerusalem! I saw that this girl was dancing with all her heart
and with all her soul and with all her might. She was
dancing her way into Jerusalem. I closed my eyes and, as
I was singing, prayed, 'Thank You, God, for helping her
enter the Holy City!'

"When I opened my eyes again, I saw that her parents were embracing and weeping and being tender to
each other. Before I knew it, Mr. Sourcream had come
over to me, threw his arms around me, and was saying,
'It's been so long! It's been so long!' Then he put his
head into my chest and began to cry. It had been so long
since his heart had been open, since he had felt any
tenderness for his wife. His daughter had opened her
parents' hearts too."[16] ⊰❦⊱

$\mathcal{D}$ancing in $\mathcal{E}$cstasy

$\mathcal{A}$ person inspired with ecstatic joy may also be inspired to dance. Dancing has always been the way of the Hasidim. And both singing and dancing are to be before God. The Baal Shem Tov said, "The dances of a Jew before his Creator are prayers," and he quoted the psalmist: "All my bones shall say: 'Lord, who is like unto You?'"[1] The Besht's great-grandson, Rebbe Nachman of Bratzlav, encouraged his Hasidim to compose prayers to recite—to be able to dance in ecstatic joy. Here is an excerpt from one of them:

> O compassionate Father, help me and make me worthy to be always joyful, so that I will merit to arouse myself always to great joy, especially on Sabbaths and holidays, and I will merit that my heart burn with fire and flame in holy joy, with great desire and longing and fervor for Your Name and Your service—until the fervor of my heart be drawn down to my feet, so that I will merit to lift my feet with great joy and I will merit to do holy dancing in great joy.[2]

The dancing of some of the Hasidic rebbes was not only ecstatic but also mystical.

Watching the Grandfather Dance

⬥ Once, Rebbe Shalom Shachna of Prohobitch visited Rebbe Arye Leib of Shpola, called the Shpoler Zeyde ["grandfather"].

On the night of the holy Sabbath, Rebbe Shalom sat at the table, as was his custom, in great awe and *d'vekut,* and he and the Shpoler Zeyde did not speak at all.

But when they had finished eating, the Grandfather said to Rebbe Shalom, "Can you dance?"

He answered, "No."

The Grandfather then said, "Watch how the Shpoler Zeyde dances!" And he immediately jumped up and began to dance around the room.

When he had danced once this way and once that way, he said, "Rebbe Shalom! Do you see the way the old man dances? Rebbe Shalom! Do you see?"

This same sequence happened a number of times, and when the dancing of the Shpoler Zeyde became even more fervent, Rebbe Shalom, who was sitting at the table in a trance of *d'vekut,* suddenly stood up and focused his gaze on him with wide-open eyes. After looking at the Shpoler Zeyde for a while this way, he turned to his Hasidim who were with him and said, "Believe me when I tell you that he has purified and sanctified his limbs to such an extent that with each step of his holy feet, he is uniting heaven and earth!"[3] ⬥

It is the Hasidic way to be happy for no apparent reason. There are many reasons, however, why a Jew who believes in God should be happy. But the point is that one does not need an excuse to sing and dance. The Hasidim sing and dance spontaneously. While studying Torah or praying or even just doing some chore, they start dancing.

> The holy Shpoler Zeyde danced on Sabbaths and holidays, but not just then. Every occasion for a *mitzvah* and of inspiration became a time of ecstatic dancing—even while he was frying the fish that he himself cooked in honor of the holy Sabbath.[4]

All the rest of the tales in this section take place on Shabbat or on Simhat Torah, the holiday when dancing is at the fore.

The Revelation in Dancing

It is written about Rebbe Moshe Leib of Sassov:

⟫ The spectacle of his dancing on Shabbat night was like a wondrous vision not of this world. Every Sabbath evening, he put on expensive new shoes and began to dance for the honor of the Queen Sabbath. His dancing was dancing of *d'vekut*, of yearning and thirsting for God until expiration. With each and every movement, he accomplished awesome and wondrous unifications— mystically uniting heaven and earth—until the whole house was full of light. All the heavenly host of angels danced with him, a great fire flamed around him, and eye-to-eye it was seen that the *Shechinah* came to rest in his synagogue.

He would be dressed all in white, and his face was like that of an angel of God. For hours at a time, he danced in a trance, utterly divorced from all materiality, without tiring. His dancing drew to him all the Hasidim in Apta, where he was living, and they never tired of watching the revelation of the *Shechinah* that took place where he danced.[5] ❧

The Dance of Parting

Rabbi Yisrael Meir of Radin was a great rabbi of a century ago. He is popularly called the Hafetz Hayim after his most famous book, *Hafetz Hayim* [The One Who Desires Life].

❧ The Hafetz Hayim had a *yeshiva* [a Jewish academy], in his hometown of Radin. In the last year of his life, on Simhat Torah, they brought him on a chair to the yeshiva, put the chair in the center of the room, whose benches had been removed, and the yeshiva students arranged *hakafot*—they danced in circles with Torah scrolls—around their great rabbi. They danced with fervor, rapturously singing songs that rose upward to heaven.

The Hafetz Hayim's great disciple, Rabbi Elhanan Wasserman, who used to travel on foot to visit his master as a sign of devotion and reverence, danced with all the young students in a great moving circle, with all the Torah scrolls, around the Hafetz Hayim.

Suddenly, Rabbi Elhanan left the circle to stand facing his master and began to dance before him. At first, everyone else ceased dancing; for a moment, they all stood and looked as the great, heavy figure of Rabbi Elhanan, whose face was as white as snow, rose and fell, rose and fell. He was full of feeling and devotion; his face white, his eyes closed, his hands rising and falling with his body. He did not seem to be dancing in

the normal sense of the word; he was seeking to rise together with his teacher, to attach himself to those supernal worlds where his great teacher was always
found.

At one moment, he would stretch out his hands
before him, as if requesting something from his master; the next moment, his hands would fall to his sides.
He would twirl around and lift himself up again, moving slowly and continually. He would briefly open his
beseeching eyes—that were always full of a prayer of
wonder at the work of the Creator—look at his rebbe,
and close them again, to begin again his dance that
was really a prayer of Rabbi Elhanan, the holy *gaon.*

The Hafetz Hayim, who sat all this time bent over,
with his attention drawn inward, suddenly lifted his
head. Because of his great weakness, it was difficult for
him—they saw this when he lifted his head and it fell back
down—but he exerted himself to raise it again and to look
at Rabbi Elhanan. Then the Hafetz Hayim lifted his hands
and began to clap, which was very hard for him, for his
hands refused to obey him. Only with difficulty was he
able to strike one hand against the other. But everyone
felt the bond between the great rabbi and his great
student, and they saw that the Hafetz Hayim wanted to
express his joy at the holy dance of his student.

There are no words to describe the fervor that
broke out among the young men, the students of the
yeshiva. A song burst from them with great power.
The yeshiva's walls shook from their voices. In their
voices was mixed a wish to unite with these two holy

people, to be like them, if only for these few minutes;
to see them together, to absorb the images of these two
holy beings into their hearts. Each young man felt he
was dancing a heavenly dance, as if his legs had disappeared and were replaced by spiritual legs that moved
and danced without effort in a dance of eternity.

They danced for hours until they were exhausted.
Young men left the circle only when they were completely
without energy, and with the last remnants of their
strength managed to drag themselves to a corner to rest
against a wall. But their eyes remained fastened to those
two figures—one so tiny and shrunken that you almost
could not see him, just a little whiteness beneath the
black hat; and next to him, a shining white figure, over
which hovered a holy presence; a figure that seemed had
just now descended from heaven to join the dance and to
disappear into the holy fire that burned all around.

It was as if the two of them, the elderly rabbi and
the mature great student, sensed that they must part,
so that later, at a time not too distant, they would both
join all the holy ones in the Garden of Eden.[6] ⊰◈⊱

A traditional system of master and disciple allows a person of
spiritual attainment to influence and direct someone who aspires to
the same level of attainment. But only when a person has humbled
himself before someone whom he clearly recognizes as greater does
a spiritual relationship develop that fosters this kind of growth. And a
spiritual master who leads a disciple to his most cherished religious
goals evokes the strongest feelings of love and reverence.

Rabbi Elhanan Wasserman took leave from his great elderly
master the Hafetz Hayim with an ecstatic dance of love. And the young

yeshiva students who watched and also danced could see clearly before them the models to which they aspired. And that vision of hope brought them great joy.

The Dance of Holy Friendship

⟳ It was close to midnight on the evening of Simhat Torah. Rabbi Avraham Yeshaya Karelitz, the great Hazon Ish [called after his famous book, "Vision of a Man"], Torah leader of the previous generation, was leaving the Ponovezh Yeshiva in Bnei Brak, Israel. Although advanced in years, he had sung and danced with all his might, rejoicing in the Torah. As he walked home with his students, he saw a man sitting on a bench, weeping openly. The man was clearly a religious Jew, but his dress and appearance seemed out of place in that neighborhood.

"My dear friend, what's wrong?" the Hazon Ish asked gently.

The man was startled by the great rabbi's presence. "Rebbe," he cried, "I'm so lonely! I'm a convert to Judaism, and I don't know anyone in town. I feel that I don't belong and that there's no place I can go to celebrate over the Torah."

The Hazon Ish thought for a moment and then said, "My friend, if you'll sing, I'll dance for you."

The man began to sing, quietly at first, then louder. The tones of his singing told of his love of Torah, of God, and of the Jewish people.

And there, in the middle of the street, the Hazon Ish began to dance. As the man's voice rose in joy, the Hazon Ish danced with ever more beauty and grace—back and forth across the sidewalk, his hands outstretched, as a man traditionally dances before a bride and groom at a wedding to cause them to rejoice.

Slowly, a crowd of people gathered around to behold the sight—the leader of the generation dancing before the convert.

Finally, the man stopped singing. "Rebbe, bless you. You've given me back my soul."[7] ⋖⋗

Dancing with God

⋖⋗ During the Holocaust, a group of young Jews were about to be sent to the gas chamber in Auschwitz. The Nazis had put them in an adjacent room where the Jews' ornaments and clothes were taken and the valuable gold teeth were removed from their mouths.

While they were waiting for what would happen, some of these young Jewish men remembered that it was Simhat Torah that day. "It's Simhat Torah," they said, "so we have to rejoice! We don't have a Torah scroll to dance with; we don't even have a printed copy of the Five Books of Moses or a prayer book with us. But the Creator of the world is with us, so we can dance with Him!"

They then all began to dance, so to speak, with God Himself.[8] ⋖⋗

Lost in a World of Delight

cstasy entails self-forgetfulness. In ecstasy, a person becomes lost in the delight of his prayer, in his Torah study, or in any other meditative religious activity. By throwing himself fully into his worship or devotion, he forgets his ego and petty concerns; he also forgets his pain and suffering. When one enters fully into sacred studying or praying, one loses oneself but finds one's larger and truer self, one's soul; one finds the true reality—God—and the ecstatic joy of Being.

Forgetfulness

Rebbe Meshullam Feish Levi of Tosh said, "If a person merits to be in the presence of a great tzaddik, all his physical and bodily desires are nullified. Because the sweetness and pleasure from experiencing the presence of the *Shechinah* is greater than any bodily pleasure. In earlier generations, there were tzaddikim who were totally divorced from material and bodily pleasures because they experienced the light of God." (It is not that bodily pleasures are unworthy but that they are beneath notice, a lesser light nullified in a greater light.) Then the Rebbe of Tosh told this tale about Rebbe Uri of Strelisk, who was called "the Seraph" because he prayed with the fervor of a fiery angel.

≈≥ Once, some people asked Rebbe Uri of Strelisk why he did not bestow the blessing of livelihood on his Hasidim, as he did for all those who came to receive his blessing—because most of the Strelisker Hasidim were very poor and needy. The rebbe replied that his Hasidim did not want material things, and "if they do want wealth, I'll give it to them. Just let them do this: during the morning service, when I'm reciting the prayer 'And David blessed the people,' when they hear me say the words 'wealth and honor are before You and You rule over everything,' let them pull on the end of my coat so that I'll remember to pray to God for them, that He bestow on them wealth."

When the Hasidim heard about this, they discussed the matter among themselves and decided to do as the rebbe said, so that they would not suffer anymore from the severe poverty and neediness that they lived with.

But during the praying, when they came to "And David blessed the people" not a single one of the Hasidim remembered to pull on the rebbe's coat, because they had completely forgotten about this world. They were truly such holy and devout people that they experienced the sweetness of prayer, which meant that all their attachment to worldly and bodily pleasures was totally nullified then because of their great *d'vekut* with God.' ≈≥

No One Noticed

≈≥ Rebbe Binyamin Zev of Lvov was a disciple of Rebbe Uri of Strelisk, and his praying too was like that of a seraph, a fiery angel. Rebbe Zev had a meeting house for his *minyan* [congregation], a single room in the upper market in the middle of the city.

Once, the mayor of Lvov was in that part of town, and he heard a roar of loud voices from many people, from Rebbe Zev and his Hasidim, because they prayed with great *d'vekut* and fervor, and he asked his aides, "What is this? What's going on here?" They told him that a rebbe and his Hasidim pray here and are shouting their prayers day and night. The mayor was upset that they were making such a racket in the middle of the town, right in the middle of the marketplace, and he sent Rebbe Zev a letter telling him to find another place to pray, away from the central areas of the city. He had to move; he could not stay here. The mayor did not want the sound of their loud prayers to be a constant din and roar in the center of town, on the streets and in the market.

But when Rebbe Zev and his Hasidim received the letter—which was written in German—not understanding German, they simply stuck it somewhere and forgot about it. Of course, they did not read it and had no idea what was in it. They continued *davvening* where they were, as always.

Some time later, when the mayor was again in that part of town and saw that the Hasidim had ignored his order, he left and came back with a group of police. They walked into the synagogue in the middle of prayers, took the Torah scroll from the Ark, and walked out—because he had threatened them that he would do this in his letter.

Rebbe Zev and his Hasidim were praying wrapped in their *tallises* and immersed in *d'vekut,* and not one of them noticed what had happened! They had no idea that someone had come in and removed the scroll from the Ark.

When they came to the Torah reading and the opening of the Ark and were singing *Binsoa HeAron* ["As the Ark Was Moved"], they saw that the Torah scroll was missing! So they searched for it and asked around outside, and that is how they found out what the mayor had written and what had happened![2] ◆

Ravished

◆ Rabbi Avigdor, the head of the religious court of Dukla, was the brother of the Tzanzer Rebbe. He was by nature someone who delved deeply into the Torah when he studied.

Immediately after Shabbat one Saturday night during the summer, while he was reviewing a certain talmudic tractate, he went out for a stroll and continued studying from memory. He was so immersed in his study that he ended up walking to the adjacent town of Vishinka, two or three miles away.

Before dawn, Reb Lazar of Vishinka went out onto the street to open up his store, and to his surprise, he saw the Rabbi of Dukla walking there. Reb Lazar could see from the rabbi's clothes that he had wandered there unintentionally.

Rabbi Avigdor, who had not yet realized where he was, saw Reb Lazar and, recognizing him, asked him in surprise, "What are you doing here in Dukla, Reb Lazar?"

"Rabbi," answered Reb Lazar, "you're now in Vishinka!"

Reb Lazar took the rabbi into his home and immediately rented a carriage to take him back to his home in Dukla.

This is what is called, "In her love [love for the Torah] will you be ravished always."³ ⚜

Holy people may go into trance not only while praying but also during intense meditation in Torah study. They are lost in the ecstasy of divine wisdom and knowledge.

Living with the Times

In 1941, Rebbe Yosef Yitzchok Schneersohn of Lubavitch related the story of an event that had taken place fifty years earlier, when he was a child of eleven.

⚜ It was early in the morning of Shabbat in which the Torah portion of *Lech Lecha* is read, still before the morning prayers, when I entered the room of my father [Rebbe Sholom Dov Ber of Lubavitch]. I found him sitting at his table in very high spirits, reviewing the Torah portion of the week. Tears were streaming from his eyes. I was very confused, for I was unable to understand how the two—an elated mood and tears—came together. But I did not dare ask.

That Shabbat morning, as every Shabbat, father prayed till late. As was his custom during winter Sabbaths when the days are short, he made *kiddush* after praying and then—instead of immediately eating—went on to pray the afternoon prayers. After that, shortly before sunset, he sat down to the Shabbat meal.

After Shabbat, father would test me on what I had studied during the week and on the *mishnayot* [ancient rabbinic teachings] I had memorized and reviewed by heart. If he was satisfied, he would present me with a gift—either a story, whose moral he would point out and explain, or a manuscript of a discourse he had delivered on Hasidic teaching. This was our arrangement in the winter of 1891.

The same took place the evening following that Shabbat *Lech Lecha.* Father tested me and then gave me a discourse about Hanukkah as a gift. I very much wanted to know why Father had been weeping, yet in such an elevated mood, when reviewing the Torah portion that morning. I stood there in confusion, unable to decide whether I should ask or not. Father noticed my confusion and said to me, "Why do you stand there like that? If you wish to say something, say it." I decided to ask.

Father answered me: "They were tears of joy." He explained, "Once, in the early years of his leadership, Rebbe Shneur Zalman of Liadi [the first Lubavitcher Rebbe], told his Hasidim, 'One must live with the times.' The younger Hasidim asked their elders what the rebbe's statement meant.[4] The elder Hasidim discussed the matter among themselves and struggled to understand the meaning. Finally, Rebbe Shneur Zalman's brother, Rabbi Yehuda Leib, explained what the rebbe meant.

"One must live with the times" means that every day, one should live with and experience in one's own life the Torah portion of the week and the specific section of the week's portion that is connected to that day.[5] The rebbe's Hasidim studied daily the section of the Torah with Rashi's commentary. The rebbe was telling them, 'One must live with the times. One must not only study the daily Torah portion but also experience it and feel it in one's own life that day.'

"The very first Torah portion of *Bereshit,* Genesis," continued my father, "is a happy portion. It includes the story of God creating the world and all its creatures and being satisfied 'that it is good.' But the ending, which describes the corruption of humanity and God's regret at creating humans [leading to the Flood] is not so pleasant. Still in all, it is a generally happy Torah portion, and in all Jewish communities there is joy and delight that we have begun the Torah anew, from the beginning.

"With the next week's reading, the portion *Noah,* comes the Flood. It is a depressing week but with a happy ending: our father Abraham is born.

"But the truly joyous week," Father concluded, explaining his mood that morning, "is *Lech Lecha.* Every day of that week's Torah portion we are living our lives together with Abraham! We are together with Abraham, who was the first to sacrifice himself to bring the message of Godliness to the world. We are together with Abraham, who bequeathed his self-sacrifice for God—for Torah and *mitzvot*—as an inheritance to each and every Jew! That's why I was weeping—for joy."[6] ⤛⤜

$\mathcal{E}$ating in $\mathcal{E}$cstasy

$\mathcal{S}$abbath and holiday feasts are sacred meals. But holy people eat all their meals in a sanctified way. During a holy meal, one keeps one's mind directed continuously, without interruption, to holiness and to God, as much as possible. The meal is surrounded before and after by blessings made over the food, the eating is intermixed with recitations and singing, and the food itself is consumed meditatively. A holy meal means eating devotionally, just as when praying.

Holy meals go back to biblical times. The altar in the ancient Temple was the "table" in God's House, on which His "house servants" (the priests) offered His "food" (sacrifices). Many of the sacrifices were eaten meditatively by the priests at sacred meals. In a vision, the prophet Ezekiel was shown the heavenly Temple of the future and its altar. The angel said, "This is the table that is before the Lord."[1] The Rabbis say that now that the ancient Temple is no longer in existence and the future Temple does not yet exist, a Jew's table must be an altar, a table at which God is present.

Rabbi Yaakov Koppel Dances
Before the Table

⌘⌘ The Baal Shem Tov once spent Shabbat in the
town of Kolomaya, and on the night of Shabbat, he
sensed the presence in the town of a holy soul radiating great light. So he went out for a stroll to find that
light. When he passed by a certain home, he saw
the light radiating from it; he also heard, within, the
sounds of singing and dancing. Seeing that the door
was slightly ajar, he went in and saw Rabbi Yaakov
Koppel dancing in ecstasy before his Sabbath table,
which was laden with good food.

Rabbi Yaakov Koppel sang and danced for a long
time until he finally stopped and noticed the Baal
Shem Tov. He welcomed his guest warmly, and the
Besht asked him, "Why do you sing and dance this
way before eating?"

Rabbi Yaakov Koppel answered, "Before I partake
of the physical food, I first stand in front of the table
and absorb the food's spiritual essence. Sometimes I
become so aroused that I sing and dance."[2] ⌘⌘

What is the food's "spiritual essence"? It is its divine aspect.
A Jewish mystic meditates on how the food has been created and is
being kept in existence (like all created things) every minute by
God's will. And a person's profound realization that God has created
this food to nourish and provide for him leads him to mystic joy.

A Holy Meal in a Sukkah in Tiberias

The following is a personal reminiscence.

⬦⬦ When I arrived in Israel many years ago for an extended first visit, I studied in an *ulpan,* an intensive Hebrew language school, in Jerusalem. The first vacation we had was for Sukkot. Most of the students went south to the Sinai Desert, which was then in Israeli hands. That was appropriate, because in the biblical story, the Jews had been in the Sinai during the time of Sukkot.

But this was my first visit to Israel, and I had not seen the country, so I traveled north to Galilee and went to Tiberias for the holiday. When I arrived, I set out to look for a synagogue, which I found. Then I searched for a place to stay and, fortunately, found a room to rent for a few days a couple of blocks away.

The next morning, I went to the synagogue for the morning prayers. Inside, I saw among the men there one unusual-looking person, a man of about sixty, burly, with graying hair, a beard, and *payot* to his shoulders; he had on a gray smock.

After services, I asked someone who the rabbi was. My idea was to ask the rabbi to arrange for someone to invite me to eat in his *sukkah.* But I was told that this synagogue at this time had no rabbi.

Oy! What was I to do? I couldn't ask someone else directly; it would be like inviting myself to his house! In a quandary, I drifted out to the street, not knowing what to

do. Then the burly man in the gray smock came over to
me on the sidewalk and asked me, "What do you want?"

At that time, my Hebrew was not good, but it was
adequate. I said, "I was looking for the rabbi, but I
found that there is no rabbi here."

He said again, more impatiently, "What do you
want?"

I stammered, because if I told him, it would be
inviting myself to his house. But finally, I just had to
tell him, "I thought the rabbi could help me find a
sukkah to eat in."

"You can be in my *sukkah*," he said.

"Great," I replied.

"But the food is not too good," he said.

"That's OK," I said. "I'm not coming for the food."

After the services that night, he took me to his
house a few blocks away and to the *sukkah* behind
his house. It was a beautiful little *sukkah*. I remember
the colorful fabric covering its walls—parakeet green,
bright red and blue—which were lovingly decorated
with pictures of the Second Temple, of the great kabbalist Rabbi Shimon bar Yohai, and so on.

We sat down and were served food by my host's
wife, an elderly woman with pure white hair. There was
not that much to eat.

But it turned out that this was just the first of ten
courses. I had thought it was the whole meal! When he
had told me the food was not too good, he had been test-
ing me, to see what sort of customer he had.

But throughout the whole meal, particularly between courses, my host—who, I found out, was a Breslover Hasid whose grandfather had come to Israel in the first wave of Hasidim in the 1800s—was reciting the *Seder Ushpizin,* the "Order of the Holy Guests," from a kabbalistic prayer book. According to tradition, a mystic guest visits the *sukkah* each of the seven nights of the holiday: Abraham, Isaac, Jacob, Moses, Aaron, David, Joseph. My host was also singing many Hasidic *niggunim* [melodies], some of which I knew and sang along with and others that I picked up. He also danced ecstatically in the *sukkah* during the meal, and I danced with him.

When studying Hasidism, I had often read about a holy meal but had never truly experienced one until then. Although we ate a gigantic meal of many courses, the physicality of the meal was so interrupted and infused with spirituality—recitations, songs, dancing—that the spirituality overwhelmed the physicality and absorbed it. The meal was totally elevated into the spiritual realm. I ate a mountain of food, but the experience was totally spiritual—a holy meal indeed.

I was in awe of my host, who, it was evident, was a great "hidden tzaddik,"[3] a person whose holiness is concealed from the eyes of men; after all, here was this holy man, and instead of being famous and surrounded by hundreds of devoted followers, he is eating alone in his *sukkah* with only one humble guest. Toward the end of the meal, I was sitting on a stool with my elbow on

the table in the *sukkah* and resting my head on my
hand. I was thinking, "This is a great hidden tzaddik.
If I only had the vessels to receive from him, who knows
what I could learn from such a person!" Then I thought,
"What did I do to merit being with him in his *sukkah?*"

At that very moment, he turned to me and said,
"I don't know how I merited to have such a guest in my
sukkah!"

I almost fell off the stool. Later I realized that in
the *Seder Ushpizin*, the first night's guest is Abraham,
and this holy kabbalist was treating me as if I were
Abraham—a great and worthy guest indeed!

Some years ago, about twenty years after the
event, I discovered who my host was. I was visiting
friends in Boston over Passover and during one meal
(not a *seder*), I was a guest at the home of some friends
of my friends, a couple who had returned to Judaism
many years ago and became Breslover Hasidim, a wonderful couple, creative and loving. We were sitting at
the table, and I happened to tell the story about the
hidden tzaddik I had met in Tiberias. My host asked me
if I remembered his name. I said, "Yes, but only the first
name, Yisrael."

My host continued, "Would you recognize him if
you saw him?"

"Yes," I answered.

"Take that blue book from the shelf near you."

Right next to me, within arm's reach, was a small
bookcase. I turned around without leaving my chair,

took out the blue book, and looked at the picture on the cover. It was my holy host from years ago in the *sukkah*. He was Rabbi Yisrael Ber Odesser, a famous Breslover Hasid now deceased but revered in Israel as an awesome tzaddik. ❧

Happiness Even While Suffering

To progress spiritually, a person must strive to deepen his faith in divine providence and to trust in God totally and implicitly. Everything that happens in the world and to each person—in even the smallest details of his daily life—occurs because God wills it. What is good comes from God, and so does what is "bad." But since God is good and acts only from love, there really is nothing bad. If a person *truly* believes this, he enters another spiritual realm and experiences great joy.

The Rabbis teach that when something bad happens to a person, he should remind himself of his faith in divine providence by saying, "Everything that the Merciful One does is for good." The Talmud praises pious people whose love for God is so strong that they rejoice even when He brings them suffering, and it applies to them the verse "Those who love Him shall be as the sun when it comes out in full strength."[1] How can someone rejoice in suffering? By transcending the lower realm of dualities—of good and bad, pleasure and pain, worldly happiness and sadness—to enter the higher realm of God's closeness, the World of Joy. Only then can one truly experience the Divine Sunlight in full strength.

The Old Man Coughing

≈ A rabbi was once in a synagogue (not his own) to pray, when a very old man sitting there began to cough. The coughing got worse until it attracted everybody's attention. The people around him did what people usually do in such situations—they brought him some water, patted him on the back, and so on—but it did not help. His coughing became so bad that his whole body was being racked. They were all worried, for he was a very frail old man. Who knew what could happen? He was coughing so severely that (God forbid) he could drop dead right there in front of them.

He coughed like that, terribly, for five minutes.

Then he stopped coughing. But after a moment, he began to laugh ecstatically!

Have you ever laughed ecstatically? It is not like belly-laughing at a good joke. It is laughter that comes from an experience of joy so great it cannot be contained. Perhaps you have seen someone laugh ecstatically once or twice in your life. It is rare, but it happens.

This old man laughed that way for five minutes and then stopped.

Of course this was amazing. To cough that way and then laugh like that? The rabbi who witnessed this was amazed. He asked the old man, "Please tell me, what was this all about?"

The old man answered, "I'll tell you my story. When I was a boy of seven in Galicia, I developed a terrible cough. When it began, it would go on and on without stopping. My mother took me to a number of doctors, but they couldn't help. Finally, she decided to take me to the Shinover Rebbe, Rabbi Yehezkel Shraga of Shinova, to ask him to pray for me or to help me in some other way.

"When she brought me in to the rebbe's room, she began to tell him about my problem. But while she was speaking to him, I began to cough, and my cough got worse and worse until my whole body was shaking.

"Suddenly, the rebbe turned to me, stamped his foot on the floor, and said, 'Little boy! Stop coughing! There'll be time enough to cough when you're eighty years old!'

"I immediately stopped coughing. And I've never had a problem with a cough for my whole life . . . until fifteen minutes ago.

"But then I realized—I'm eighty years old! . . . So I began to laugh!"[2] ᐊᐃᐧᐳ

Why was he laughing? It certainly was not pleasant for him to be afflicted again by this terrible cough! But the miracle he experienced proved to him that there is a God. And if a person knows there is a God, no matter what his sufferings are, he is still laughing.

Poverty and Bliss

ᐊᐃᐧᐳ Rabbi Shimshon of Uzriyan visited Rabbi Hayim of Chernovitz, but he did not find the rabbi at home, so he went to the synagogue, where the rabbi was studying Torah.

When Rabbi Hayim saw Rabbi Shimshon, he was thrilled at this unexpected visit and invited Rabbi Hayim home to offer him a meal.

But when the rebbetzin saw that her husband had brought back a guest, she became angry and yelled at him, "Why do you bring home guests when there is no food in the house to serve them?" They were so terribly poor, there was no food in the house. The rabbi replied gently, asking her not to yell and explaining that this was a very important, special guest.

Some pious Jews, during the morning prayers, not only put on the Rashi *tefillin* that all men wear but, for the concluding part of the prayer service, replace them with a second kind called Rabbeinu Tam *tefillin*. Rabbi Hayim gave these other *tefillin* of his to someone to pawn so that he would have a little money to buy something to eat.

When that was taken care of, the rebbetzin served the rabbi and his guest, bringing to the table one roll and one bowl of soup, with a single wooden spoon.

When Rabbi Shimshon saw this poverty, he refused to eat. There was not even enough for his host! But Rabbi Hayim begged him to eat with him and promised that the one bowl of soup would be enough for both of them. "We'll divide it," he said. "You'll eat one spoonful, then I'll eat one, and so on." And that is what they did.

Rabbi Shimshon was not used to this kind of poverty. And to eat with one wooden spoon, from one clay bowl! But because he did not want to insult the rabbi, of whom he was so fond, he ate. And he experienced a revelation.

Years later, whenever Rabbi Shimshon told about this meal he shared with the holy and pure Rabbi Hayim of Chernovitz, he would say, "I can still savor in my mouth the unbelievable taste of the meal I ate with Rabbi Hayim, because I tell you, that was actually the taste of the Garden of Eden."³ ✎

When a person sees everything that happens to him, good or "bad," as coming directly from God and therefore as certainly good, he enters the mystic state of consciousness called the Garden of Eden. Rabbi Shimshon at first pitied the Chernovitzer for his poverty, but he made a mistake. The Chernovitzer was terribly poor—he lived in a broken-down cottage and did not have enough to eat—but he really dwelt in the Garden of Eden of nearness to God and of mystic joy. When sharing food with such a holy person, one tastes, if only briefly, what he tastes, as the psalm says, "Taste and see that the Lord is good; happy is the person who trusts in Him."⁴

The Rebbe of Azarov's White Beard

✎ The son and daughter of two well-known rabbis were being married, and Rebbe Yehiel of Azarov, who was related to both families, attended the wedding. He brought with him a group of his Hasidim. At the party, they led the festivities, since Hasidim specialize in joy—in singing and dancing. During the dancing, the rebbe himself led the singing and was accompanied by the musicians who were present.

When everyone was exhausted from the dancing and sat down to rest for a while, the rebbe also sat down and, taking hold of his pure white beard, began to speak to those around him. He said, "You can see how white my beard is. But I tell you, these white hairs did not come from age"—for the rebbe was not that old. Then he began to recount all the sufferings and difficulties he had undergone in his life until everyone there was weeping. But the rebbe's face showed not the least sign of pain or distress as he spoke.

When he finished speaking, a smile began to spread over his holy face, and he loudly and joyfully called out to the musicians the words of the psalm: "Sing to Him, with music, telling of all His wondrous deeds!"[5]

With the tears still drying on their cheeks, everyone jumped up with joy, and the ecstatic dancing began once again.[6] ❧

The rebbe's beard had prematurely turned white because of the many troubles he had endured, sufferings that were so severe that even hearing about them made others weep. Yet his faith in God was so strong that he could recount his sufferings calmly and afterward make himself and others rejoice and sing praises to the living God for all His wondrous deeds. Why did the rebbe recount his troubles publicly? To teach everyone there, and us too, a great lesson in joy.

The World of Pure Joy

❧ Rebbe Hayim of Tzanz suffered greatly from a foot problem. Finally, he needed an operation. Since the operation was very painful, the doctor wanted to give him an injection and put him to sleep. The doctor said, "I have to give you an injection; the operation's very painful."

"I'll make a deal with you," said Rebbe Hayim. "You don't have to give me an injection. Just do what you have to do, and let me do what I have to do. But I have to ask one favor. If I don't open my eyes after the operation's over, don't disturb me. I may lie on the operating table for a few more hours. But promise me that you won't disturb me."

The doctor promised him.

Then Rebbe Hayim closed his eyes and looked as if he were not in this world. After the operation was over, the doctor said, "There are hardly any signs of life in his body. I'm afraid that he's close to death."

Rebbe Hayim's children said, "Don't worry. If our father said everything will be fine, it will be; trust him."

For the next four hours, Rebbe Hayim lay on the operating table, seemingly lifeless. Then he opened his eyes and said, "Was the operation successful?"

After telling him, the doctor said, "I hope you don't mind my asking you, but what did you do?"—because the doctor was amazed that during the operation, Rebbe Hayim showed no signs of pain at all.

Rebbe Hayim replied, "I have to tell you something that my holy master, Rebbe Naftali of Ropshitz, taught me. We all know how to feel joy on a worldly level. We need a reason to feel joy. If something very good happens, we're joyful. My master, the Ropshitzer, taught me that I can be joyful for no reason. He said that one cannot always be in that place, but when you're there, you must really be there. So when I knew that I was going to have a lot of pain, I simply elevated myself to a state of pure joy. But because I had to be there fully, I couldn't come back right away."[7]

Revived by a Song

This story tells why Rabbi Mordechai Yaffeh wrote the famous Sabbath hymn "*Mah Yafit*" (How Beautiful).

↝ Rabbi Mordechai, who was the religious judge of the town of Horodna, had an only son who was a very special boy. This boy was once traveling on a road near Horodna and was murdered. The lord of the town then went to see the crime scene and ordered the townspeople to take the body to a nearby hotel that he owned until it could be buried. So they put the body in a room, closed the windows, and locked the door.

The boy's father, Rabbi Mordechai Yaffeh, knew nothing of this until *erev* Shabbat, just before Shabbat began. When they told him, he resolved not to grieve on the Sabbath, because the Sabbath is a day of joy, and it is forbidden to grieve on the holy day for any reason. So Rabbi Mordechai exerted himself to accomplish this, but he was not able to, until he began to compose the hymn, which begins "*Mah yafit u'mah na'amt ahava beta'anugim, at Shabbat mesos nugim,*" "How beautiful and pleasant you are with delights, O Shabbat, joy of the grieving." He cleaved to this thought with great strength and with all his heart until he completely forgot what had happened to his son and his grief. The ecstasy of Shabbat joy inspired by his song made him completely forget his sorrow.

This caused a great commotion in heaven: How was it possible for a human to reach such a level, to push off such grief, out of love and yearning for the holy Sabbath? So when Rabbi Mordechai came to the words *chai zakof mach,* "O Living One, let the lowly rise, alive," it was agreed in heaven to revive his son and decreed that the dead and departed should rise up to life. And so heaven restored the soul to his son's body. This happened on the night of the Sabbath.

When the boy awoke, he wanted to leave by the door, but it was locked. He considered what to do. Should he remain there? He was afraid that perhaps he was still among his murderers.[8] He decided to force his way out of the window. But once outside, he thought, "I'm outside the Sabbath limits of the city"; since Jewish law forbids travel on Shabbat, he could not enter the city. So he fled into the woods nearby and was there for the rest of the Sabbath.

But immediately after sundown on Saturday night, he ran to the town and to his father, just when his father was about to remove his shoes in mourning and sit *shiva.* When Rabbi Mordechai saw his son, he thought that the whole story about his son's death was false, but his son told him that the story was true and that he had heard in the upper world that because of his father's Sabbath hymn "*Mah Yafit,*" they had decided in heaven to revive him.

When the lord heard about the boy's body disappearing, he went to the hotel manager, who told him that the boy had been revived from the dead and had gone to his father, Rabbi Mordechai, and was at his house. And the boy told him too the whole story. After that, the hymn "*Mah Yafit*" became popular with the gentiles too, who had seen that the Jews were always singing it.[9] ⫸

Joy and Ecstasy Remove Suffering

⫷ In 1806, when Rebbe Nachman of Bratzlav was very sick, his infant son, Shlomo Ephraim, who was a little over a year old, died. While he was sitting *shiva,* Rebbe Nachman said, "After all these afflictions, nevertheless, God, blessed be He, is still good to us. Although I don't want to minimize the afflictions—for in truth they're not minor afflictions—but by clinging to God in *d'vekut* one attains an ecstatic joy that removes any suffering. In fact, through the afflictions themselves, a person can come closer to God, blessed be He, and achieve *d'vekut,* for who takes a person's health? God, blessed be He. By that realization, I come closer to Him and cling to Him. When He takes, God forbid, one of my children, who takes him? God, blessed be He. If that is so, I'm now closer than ever to Him, blessed be He."[10]

Four years later, on a Sabbath night in 1810, there was a big fire in the streets close to Rebbe Nachman's home; house after house was going up in flames. Rebbe Nachman was sitting with his Hasidim at his Sabbath table, and they asked him to teach Torah. "I know nothing!" he replied, as was his way. [Rebbe Nachman taught that the essence of knowledge is to know that one does not know, and to rise in spiritual wisdom, he

passed again and again through higher and higher
levels of "not knowing."]

   Just then a number of people ran in, in great confusion, yelling that everyone had to leave because the
very next street was on fire. When the rebbe heard this,
his holy face became very red, and he said, "*Shoyn,
shoyn*"—meaning "I knew already!"—because the rebbe
had predicted there would be a fire and had spoken
about it."¹¹

   Rebbe Nachman then immediately left the house,
and there was great confusion at the table. All the Hasidim tried to save whatever they could from his house.
The rebbe went to the synagogue, where they brought
him a fur coat, so he would not be cold, since he was sick
and weak. He then went by himself across the small
river, walking in the water. Then he climbed a hill outside the town of Bratzlav that overlooked the synagogue
and his house. From there he gazed down on the town and
on his home, which with many others was burning.

   When his great disciple Rabbi Noson saw that
the rebbe went alone in the direction of the hill, he
too helped the other Hasidim remove things from the
rebbe's house. They also saved the Torah scrolls from
the synagogue and the *beit midrash* [the adjacent study
hall]. But while that was going on, Rabbi Noson left
the others and ran after the rebbe. He found Rebbe
Nachman sitting, in great joy, viewing his burning
home. "What would I have done," said the rebbe, "if
my house had been spared while so many other houses
had burned and everyone else in town was suffering

such grief? But now, 'He [God and the rebbe] is with them in their trouble.'[12] But in truth, this isn't any suffering at all, for everything is from Him, blessed be He." That is all he said; then he simply sat there, in intense *d'vekut* and great joy.[13]

Rebbe Nachman's house was completely burned in this fire, and as a result of this and for other reasons, he decided, a few days later, to leave Bratzlav and to move to Uman. The townspeople and the Hasidim who lived in Bratzlav were heartbroken. When they were sitting in the coach, leaving Bratzlav, Rebbe Nachman said to Rabbi Noson, "It's fitting to leave them, because it's not right that they should be suffering so much when I am so joyful. If they had been burned out and not me, I would have to suffer with them, for when any Jew is suffering like this, I too would have to bear his pain and suffer with him. But now that my home too is destroyed, I have to accept the divine decree with love and joy, and for that one needs great joy, to overcome the feeling of affliction with very great joy. So it's not right that I should be here with them, when they're miserable and they should have to see me so joyful."

The rebbe elevated to supreme levels of ecstatic joy in order to transcend his sense of suffering and loss. Yet since he simply could not contain his joy, he felt that seeing him in that condition was actually an affront to the townspeople, who could not understand or attain such awesome spiritual levels.[14]

Later Rebbe Nachman said, "One needn't even mention money losses, which I of course accept with

joy, for it says, 'Skin for skin; everything a man has, he
will give to save himself.'¹⁵ But even if, God forbid, I lose
a member of my family, may God, blessed be He, protect
me today and in the future; that too I'd accept with love
and great joy, so much so that I'd have to force myself to
perform all the customs of mourning, such as weeping
and so on, because I would be in a state of great joy
then, since everything is equal to me, as if nothing had
happened."¹⁶ ⊰⊱

Rebbe Nachman's comment about the verse, "Skin for skin,"
means that he was willing to give up everything he owned to save
himself, that is, to retain his joy and bliss.

From My Naked Flesh
I Would See God!

The tormented Job cried out, "But while I am still alive, though my
skin is torn from me, yet from my naked flesh I would see God! O
that I might see Him for myself; that *my* eyes, and not those of another, might behold Him. For that, how do I long!"¹⁷

Job, who was righteous in all his ways, suffered from the deaths
of his children, the destruction of his property, and a severe disease.
Yet when he cried out, "Why?" God answered him from a whirlwind
and said, essentially, "Where were you when I created the world? Do
you know how I created even one blade of grass?" Although God
never explained to Job the reason for his suffering, the very fact that
He revealed Himself was answer enough for Job, for if we are truly certain that God exists, our doubts and questions dissipate.

The following tale was told by a Gerer Hasid who survived
Auschwitz, the Kingdom of Death, and reached Jerusalem, the cap-
ital of the Kingdom of Eternal Life. The story shows that closeness

to God produces the greatest bliss and delight and that a human being can overcome the most horrifying circumstances, even the terrors of the Holocaust.

⁂ With his father and mother, two brothers, and three sisters, a young Hasid arrived at Auschwitz on one of the trains, in a cattle car. In a short while, they were all standing on the platform in the same terrifying "selection" line, supervised by the wicked persecutor, Dr. Mengele, deciding, in the phrase of the Yom Kippur prayers about each year's decree, "whom to life and whom to death." To the right was to life; to the left, to death. Everyone in his family—his parents, his brothers, and his sisters—was sent to the left, to death; he alone was sent to the right, to work doing slave labor for the Nazis.

But before he and the seventeen other young men who were assigned to his slave labor unit were given permission to work, they were humiliated by being disinfected. They were marched to a pool and ordered to strip off their clothes and jump naked into the water. Their clothes would be burned, and they would don camp uniforms. The water in the pool contained a large amount of carbolic acid, a caustic disinfectant of the sharpest kind. It is hard to describe the burning effect it produces on all the parts of the body, especially when it penetrates the ears and eyes.

All of the young men jumped into the water and immediately jumped out. "But I," said this young man, "stayed in that burning water for a long moment while I turned to God and prayed, 'Master of the world! I had a mother and father, two brothers, and three sisters; now I have no one—no father, no mother, no brothers, no sisters! I had at least clothes to cover my body, but now I don't have even that. They've stripped me of my clothes and left me naked, as I stand before You. If I have nothing left, do I not then see You, Master of the world? As it says, "From my naked flesh I would see God!" I am with You, and You are with me, and that no one can take from me! If so, what do I lack?'

"At the moment I had these thoughts," he said as he finished his tale, "I began to feel a delight so profound that I have never experienced anything like it in my whole life, either before or since. My comrades in suffering who were standing by the side of the pool were yelling to me, 'Why are you standing there in that fiery water? Hurry, get out of that hell!'

"But while they were shouting to me, I was lost in my thoughts. I was in heaven itself and enjoying the unutterable bliss of the experience that God, blessed be He, was with me."[18] ⊰⊱

Reb Arele's Sukkot

This Holocaust story was told at a Sukkot meal eaten in a *sukkah* on Mount Zion by Rabbi Mendel Mezakritim, who escaped from the Nazis and ended up in Jerusalem.

⊰⊱ Rabbi Mendel said that in Auschwitz, they learned on the day before Sukkot in 1943 that there would be a "selection" in the camp on the day of Sukkot. The

strong and healthy would go to the right and be allowed
to live and work. The weak, frail, and sick were sent to
the left to be exterminated. The Nazis said, "Why feed
Jews who can't work?"

You can imagine the feelings of the camp inmates.
They were terribly worried. Rabbi Mendel said he was
less worried than most, "because I was healthy and
strong. I also looked fit," he said, "so I was fairly confident that they would let me live. My concern and worry
was about Reb Arele, one of the most pious Jews in the
camp. He was so thin you could see every vertebra in
his spine. He was like a walking skeleton. He only ate
potato peels, since he refused to eat any nonkosher
food,[19] even the thin soup they served in the camp."
He was so thin, Rabbi Mendel said, that he brought to
mind the famous Rabbi Tzadok mentioned in the Talmud, who fasted for forty years to avert the destruction
of the Second Temple. Rabbi Tzadok ate only dried figs,
and it was said that he was so thin, you could see a
fig going down his digestive tract. "It was clear what
Reb Arele's fate would be in the selection," said Rabbi
Mendel, "and my heart grieved at the thought."

Not long after this brooding about Reb Arele, Reb
Arele visited Rabbi Mendel's cell in the barracks. He
was troubled and disturbed. "I tried to comfort and console him about his fate in the selection, but he quickly
disabused me of the idea that he was worried about his
own survival. His only concern was that he would not
be able to fulfill the *mitzvot* of Sukkot! With tears in
his eyes, he said, 'How can I build a *sukkah* in the

camp? And how can I fulfill the *mitzvah* of waving the Four Species—the *lulav, etrog, hadasim,* and *aravot*—palm, citron, myrtle, and willow branches? It's impossible!' Seeing how Reb Arele was only worried about how to fulfill the *mitzvot* and not about his own fate, my heart inwardly wept for him."

"On the night Sukkot began, Reb Arele came to me again," said Rabbi Mendel, "but now his face was beaming with joy. He told me he had solved the problem of how to have a *sukkah* and the Four Species! Grasping my arms in a rapture of ecstasy, he said, 'Rabbi Mendel, with God's help, I realize I now have everything I need to celebrate Sukkot with joy!' At first I thought that he had lost his mind; he was so joyful. But looking at him more closely, I realized that he was shining with the radiance of an angel of God.

"He took my hand in his and said, 'Everybody knows that there is an argument in the Talmud between Rabbi Akiba and Rabbi Eliezer about what kind of *sukkah* is meant when the Torah says, God "made you dwell in *sukkot* [booths]" [when the Jews were in the Sinai Desert]. Rabbi Akiba said it means *sukkot mamash,* actual booths. Rabbi Eliezer said it means the Clouds of Glory that accompanied the Jews in the desert, which were like divine booths hovering over them and protecting them. The Talmud also says that there were seven kinds of Clouds of Glory: regular clouds, smoke, and so on. So,' said Reb Arele, his face beaming in a smile, 'do you see, Rabbi Mendel? Aren't the clouds of smoke rising from the chimneys where they are burning our brothers and sisters Clouds of Glory? Aren't they a *sukkah* for us? The Holy One, blessed be He, used to let us build actual *sukkot,* but now He wants us to dwell in these Clouds of Glory and to rejoice in His holiday.

"'I've also decided how to fulfill the *mitzvah* of the Four Species. Everybody knows that the *Midrash* says that the *lulav,* the palm branch, symbolizes the human spine, whose shape it resembles; the myrtle symbolizes the eye, whose shape its leaf resembles; the willow leaf symbolizes the mouth, which it resembles; and the *etrog,* the citron fruit, resembles the heart. God formerly allowed us to use the different plants for the Four Species, but now He wants us to use our own bodies. If our spine bends in worship to Him alone, if our eyes are turned to Him only, if our mouths only utter His praises, and if our hearts are full of love for Him, then our bodies are like the Four Species, as it says in the prayer, "All my bones shall say, 'O Lord, who is like unto You!'"[20] And then we can offer our bodies to Him as pure sacrifices. So now,' said Reb Arele, 'I'll be able to rejoice in the holiday, as it says, "and you shall rejoice in your holidays."'

"His eyes as he said this were jumping with joy," said Rabbi Mendel, "but my eyes were flooded with tears.

"The next morning, when we stood in line for the selection, I managed to stand next to Reb Arele. He was still beaming with joy. But suddenly he seemed to become troubled. When I whispered to him, asking him what was the matter, he told me that he was worried

that his heart might not be considered a perfect *etrog*,
since it was so broken [pious Jews try to select a perfect
and unblemished *etrog* for the holiday]. When I reminded him of the teaching of Rebbe Aharon of Karlin
that to God, no heart is more perfect than a broken
heart, he once again became full of joy.

"When the Nazis shoved him to the left," said
Rabbi Mendel, "my heart almost broke from grief, but
the last words we heard on his lips were the words from
the verse: 'You shall rejoice before the Lord your God.'

"That was the Sukkot of Reb Arele."[21] ⚬⚬⚬

Joy Saves from Death

It is a traditional Jewish wedding custom for guests to individually
dance before a bride and groom, as a form of "holy entertainment,"
to cause the new couple to be glad on the day of their joy.

⚬⚬⚬ The mother of Rebbe Elimelech of Ridnick was ill
on her bed and near death. Just then, a procession with a
bride and groom passed by the house. Rebbe Elimelech
ran out, brought the bride and groom into the room
where his mother lay, and began to dance before them—
to fulfill the *mitzvah* of rejoicing a bride and groom.
Immediately his mother began to recover, and her situation improved.[22] ⚬⚬⚬

Most people at such a moment would be drawn into the mood
of death and depression that fills a room where someone is expiring. Yet instead of allowing himself to become depressed, the Rebbe
of Ridnick seized the opportunity to use the *mitzvah* of rejoicing a
bride and groom to lift himself to a state of joy. A sick person needs

to be uplifted, not for others to descend with him into sadness. The rebbe's joy pulled his mother away from the gates of death.

This tale not only teaches us how to behave with sick people but also tells us something even deeper about our own lives. God is joy; God is bliss. When we allow ourselves to fall into depression and sadness, not only are we farther from God; we are closer to death. But joy can save from death.

Only Joy, for There Is No Bad, No Trouble, No Sadness, No Death

≈◎≈ Rabbi David Leikes, a chief disciple of the Baal Shem Tov, served as the rabbi and the head of the religious court of Brody. He was held in special regard by the Holy Society, the inner circle of the Besht's close disciples, because of his outstanding Torah knowledge and his great joy and trust in God.

Although Rabbi David was diligent in Torah study, studying every free moment, his constant studying did not enfeeble him physically, as it does many others; he was a powerful and vigorous man, despite his age. He used to enjoy treating the Holy Society to drinks, which he himself brought from a tavern owned by a rich widow, who, because of her piety, did not always demand cash from the Besht's often poor disciples and even used to add some extra liquor or wine, free, when they bought from her. Although Rabbi David was a great Torah scholar, even among the inner circle, and he was also the oldest, he was not concerned about his honor and was happy to get the liquor himself, feeling that bringing the liquor or wine, which made men

happy, was a *mitzvah;* it was a task he cherished and
would not delegate to anyone else. The Baal Shem Tov
rewarded him for this holy service of his with the job
and honor of leading the dancing at every celebration,
because Rabbi David was also an outstanding dancer
whose fervor in dancing was unlimited.

Rabbi David was full of joy, and he loved to dance
at every opportunity, not just at formal celebrations.
The Hasidim said that for him, every time was a time
of celebration. If it was up to him, he would have done
away with all pious self-affliction and all weeping, and
he would have annulled all fasting, except for *Tisha
b'Av* [the fast lamenting the destruction of the ancient
Temple in Jerusalem] and Yom Kippur [the Day of
Atonement]! It was told that he even chanted the Tisha
b'Av lamentations in a cheerful melody and on Yom Kippur, when everyone is trembling and gloomy because of
the fear of judgment, even then he still had a smile on
his face, for he was always cheerful and smiling.

Rabbi David received everyone he met with a
smile, but fate did not smile at him. He had four sons
and three daughters, all of whom died suddenly, some
when young, some when adults. Then, when Rabbi
David was seventy-three, his wife passed away, and he
was left all alone, with no living descendants. But Rabbi
David did not weep or mourn or allow sadness to rule
over him for even a minute.

As a mature man, he had wept only once, many
years earlier, when the holy Baal Shem Tov passed away
and the Hasidim were orphaned of their great teacher.

Rabbi David did not cry because of the death itself but because of his sadness at the abandoned flock that now had no shepherd. Even then he wept only briefly and quickly got hold of himself and his suffering. At the end of the *shiva*, the seven days of most solemn mourning, he held a small "celebration" [*hillula*] for the elevation of the Baal Shem Tov's soul, to which Rabbi David brought some liquor for everyone. The tradition teaches that such a commemoration elevates the deceased's soul in heaven. The yearly commemoration for a great tzaddik on the anniversary of his death is called a celebration because he accomplished his purpose on earth and he has been elevated to great joy in heaven.

Rabbi David did not change character when his pious wife passed away, and he prayed the afternoon and evening services in the same way as always, with a sweet and joyful melody; he even chanted the *Kaddish* [the mourner's memorial prayer] for his wife in a voice full of joy and happiness. That was the way he acted all the seven days of the *shiva* mourning period. His face was always joyful and happy, without a moment's lapse. People said that during the *shiva*, his ever-smiling face even had a special radiance, as if, instead of needing to be consoled, he wanted to console the many people who came to share in his suffering. And indeed, his shining, cheerful face during his mourning encouraged and inspired many people not to weep about their own troubles and to uproot sadness from their hearts.

They said that within Rabbi David's realm, the evil inclination of sadness had no reign. He used to repeat in the name of his master, the Baal Shem Tov, that it is not enough to say, "This *too* is for good"—a traditional pious phrase uttered when a person suffers affliction— as if there might be a question about it, God forbid; one should say, "*This* is good." He also said in the name of the Baal Shem Tov, "The Rabbis teach that 'a person should bless God for the bad just as he blesses Him for the good,' because there *is* no bad; *bad is good.*" The holy Baal Shem Tov said, "There is no bad." Rabbi David added, "There is no suffering, no sadness."

Rabbi David's fellow townspeople knew his character and his nature, his way in joy and trust in God, and from him they learned to go through life without suffering and sadness. When they came to visit him in his mourning for his wife, to pray with him in a *minyan,* and to study Torah with him for the elevation of his wife's soul, they did not put on a sad face; they did not sigh, *"Oy vey!"* or cry out, "What a loss!" and similar expressions that come from a broken heart and break other hearts. Those who visited him did not utter a word that had any trace of consolation; they did not justify the heavenly judgment or demand that heaven rectify an injustice. They simply sat with Rabbi David and prayed and studied or discussed Torah subjects with him.

As always, Rabbi David passed on deep teachings and insights about Torah or Hasidism in the name of the Baal Shem Tov and told amazing tales about how the Besht helped those in need and repaired souls. Everything Rabbi David said brought joy to his listeners, encouraged them, and filled them with trust in God.

But none of this was known to two Torah scholars who came from a distant town to visit and console him in his time of mourning. They had heard about Rabbi David but had never met him. All they knew was that he was a great tzaddik, the last living member of the inner circle of the Baal Shem Tov's disciples. When they heard that he had lost his wife, they traveled to him from far away to fulfill with this saintly sage the *mitzvah* of comforting mourners. They also hoped, by the way, to be rewarded for their exertions by meriting to sit at his feet and to hear from him a few teachings and holy sayings of his master.

Because of the distance they traveled, they reached Ber, Rabbi David's town, on the seventh and last day of the *shiva*. Their long journey had worn them down, and they were exhausted. When they arrived and entered his home, they began to utter customary words of consolation, of sharing in the mourner's suffering, and of justifying heavenly judgment.

At first, Rabbi David went along with their well-intentioned commiseration, but when they went on and on this way, the always cheerful Rabbi David departed from his usual polite and pleasant manners and corrected the two pious sages, saying that they were not acting according to the teaching that he had received from his holy master, the Baal Shem Tov.

"The Baal Shem Tov used to say, 'A human being is so precious, even more precious than an angel or seraph! His soul is hewn from under God's Throne of Glory, and the *Shechinah* is always shining in a halo around

his head. He is like a prince, a king's son: he should
always be joyful and never experience any suffering,
because there is no bad, no trouble, no sadness, no
death.' The Rabbis say that, even when deceased, the
righteous are called 'alive.' The holy Baal Shem Tov was
summoned to the Heavenly Yeshiva, but he has not
departed from this world, he is still alive, and 'only the
living, they shall praise You!'" When this verse left
Rabbi David's mouth, it came out with a melody and
fervently, just as he used to sing it when the Baal Shem
Tov was alive and sat amid his Holy Society of close
disciples, all of them dancing around him with fervor
and flaming devotion.

As he sang, a stream of tears burst from Rabbi
David's eyes. He wept uncontrollably from his bitterness of soul and heartbrokenness. Why? Perhaps
because all the pain from the deaths of his whole family
was aroused by the words of consolation and by the
song and erupted suddenly in one great weeping. He
could no longer resist the evil inclination of sadness.
But afterward, Rabbi David was so ashamed of what he
felt was his weakness and lack of faith that he sunk
his head in remorse.

When he realized that he was in danger of falling
into a depressed mood of constricted consciousness,
the opposite of his usual exalted joyful mood of expanded consciousness, he hurried, the day after the
final day of the *shiva*, to the tavern of the pious widow
and consoled himself with some wine, for Hasidim

know how to use wine and liquor to cure their sadness. When the wine entered him, his sadness left.

But from that time on, Rabbi David resolved to fight sadness with all his energy—by Torah study and prayer, by song and music, and even—to make a distinction—by drinking liquor.

Finally, Rabbi David realized that being alone left him vulnerable to depression. So one day he went to the widow who ran the tavern, and whose name was Haya Sheintzi, and said to her, "I want to marry you."

She blushed and answered, "You are a great tzaddik and a Torah scholar. Who and what am I? A simple woman who serves drinks in a tavern, a widow without children." Then she added pointedly, "But I still hope to have children, Rabbi David, and you are quite old!"

"I promise you," replied Rabbi David, "that, God willing, we will yet merit to raise children to Torah, *huppah,* and good deeds."

Haya smiled at the reference to the customary blessing but did not give him an answer.

After some time, the pious Haya saw in a dream that the Baal Shem Tov and his disciples were dancing around her in a circle while she stood under a *huppah.* She looked this way and that in astonishment, because she saw no bridegroom. The Baal Shem Tov then pointed out to her one of his disciples, whose face was shining like the sun. She looked and saw that he resembled Rabbi David Leikes. Then the holy Baal Shem Tov whispered to her, "I promise you that you will yet have

children." When Rabbi David came to her home the next
day and told her that he had had that same dream, she
agreed to marry him. Haya married Rabbi David and
had, with him, three boys and one girl.

Rabbi David reached a ripe old age, more than one
hundred years. Every day, until his final day on earth,
a religious court convened in his home, and the judges
brought every difficult case to him for his decision.
Only for the easy cases did they rely on their own judgment. On the last day of Rabbi David's life, a very difficult case was brought before the judges, and they were
unable to reach a decision. The family did not allow
anyone to enter the rabbi's room, since his condition
was critical; he was close to death. But the raised voices
and quarrels of the opposing parties and the back-and-
forth arguments of the judges reached the ears of Rabbi
David in the next room. Since he was then alone, and he
feared that his family would not hear his voice because
of the arguments going on, he banged his hand down
on the table near his bed so powerfully that the table
broke. When some of his family rushed in, he told them
to go immediately to the room where the case was being
heard and tell everyone to come in to him.

He complained to his family, saying, "The Rabbis
say that every religious judge who judges truthfully becomes a partner to God in the work of creation. Do you
want to deprive me of that partnership?" The judges
and the parties to the dispute immediately entered his
room and laid before him all the facts and arguments of
the case, and Rabbi David then gave his judgment.

Later that day, he passed away. Just before his soul
exited, he whispered, "I'm going from one court to another"—from the earthly religious court to the Heavenly
Court.[23] ❧

An Ecstatic Passing

A tale tells of the passing of another disciple of the Baal Shem Tov.

❧ Rabbi Yitzhak HaCohen Maggid was an eminent
Torah scholar and a wealthy householder. He became,
against the views of his family, who vehemently
opposed Hasidism, one of the leading disciples and
followers of the Baal Shem Tov (his mother fainted
when she first heard of his conversion to Hasidism).
He remained a fervent Hasid all his life.

On the final day of his life, when Rabbi Yitzhak
was close to death and family, friends, and many other
people crowded around his bed, he saw that all their
faces were sad. He rebuked them, saying, "You should
be happy! As the Torah verse says, 'She laughs on her
final day.'"[24]

He then told members of his family to get the gold
and silver candlesticks and to light candles as for a holiday. He also asked them to bring musicians and singers,
to play hymns and praises of God, and to sing sweet Hasidic melodies—as he put it—"to accompany my soul,
as it leaves, with joy."

Then, in a state of *d'vekut,* of holy ecstasy and
Hasidic joy, his soul exited in holiness and purity.[25] ❧

Joy Until the Final Moment of Life

~~~ In the Yeshiva Chochmei Lublin (Academy of
the Sages of Lublin), the sacred studies were proceed-
ing in their usual order, the night shifts were studying
with fervor. As in some other holy places, students
here were organized into shifts so that the sound of
Torah study would be heard twenty-four hours a day.
The light of Tuesday morning, the week of the Torah
portion *Lech Lecha,* was dawning. The great hall of the
yeshiva was already full of students, and the sound of
loud studying could be heard from afar. Soon the great
teacher, the *gaon,* Rabbi Meir Shapiro of Lublin, would
appear. The students were waiting for him before beginning morning prayers, but the rabbi did not appear.
Then the bad news of Job went from mouth to ear:
"He's sick."

In the middle of the previous night, he had been
seen in the library bent over a book at a reading stand.
He mentioned to a student he happened to encounter
then that he had a fever and was shivering. In the
morning, his temperature rose, and he was forced to
cancel his daily morning class in the yeshiva.

Two students, both good singers, were called to
his room and at his request began to sing the prayer
"May the Lord Answer You on the Day of Your Trouble."
He had contracted diphtheria, but the doctors treating
him incorrectly diagnosed his condition.

He experienced terrible pains, and the diphtheria
constricted his throat, but a cheerful smile never left

his face, which was otherwise contorted with pain. One day and then another passed, and his condition was worsening. The doctors were calming everyone, but the hearts of hundreds of students beat with trepidation.

On Wednesday night, at two in the morning, the rabbi called to the shift of students studying in the yeshiva to come to his room and sing for him the famous song he had composed, "To Make Known and Reveal That He Is King over All the Earth," which he used to sing on the night of Yom Kippur.

Another day passed; the rabbi became increasingly weaker and his throat more choked and constricted. He could hardly speak any longer. Fear and dread hovered over hundreds of eyes full of tears: Can it be? Is it forbidden to even think that a disaster is approaching? The students asked Rabbi Meir if they should increase their prayers and recite psalms in congregation for his welfare. The rabbi refused to permit it, saying, "Don't consider me to be sick."

But that afternoon, he sent a messenger to Rabbi Shlomo Halbershtat, the head of the Lublin Jewish community and a member of the yeshiva's board, with a short note that said only, "I'm very afraid of this." Rabbi Halbershtat was taken aback and overcome with fear. After a moment's reflection, it seemed to him that the rabbi was calling him. He went to him, but the rabbi took the note from his hand and ripped it to shreds on the spot. Confused, Rabbi Shlomo ran to the great rabbi of Lublin, Rabbi Akiva Eiger, and told him what was written in the note.

The disturbing news spread with the speed of
lightning. Many Jews came to Rabbi Meir to see about
his health; the yeshiva students wanted to turn over the
world, to do everything possible, to alert Polish Jewry
and its rabbinic leaders to pray for Rabbi Meir's recov-
ery. They were preparing to go to the graves of tzaddikim in the city to pray—to the graves of the Maharal,
to the Seer of Lublin—but the rabbi forbade them. His
only anxiety was to know whether classes were contin-
uing at the yeshiva as usual. He never stopped smiling,
as if to say, "In a little while, I'll greet the *Shechinah*."
Only at dusk on Thursday did he give in to the students'
pleas and allow them to visit the graves of the tzaddikim in the cemetery to pray, as he always did, with
the simple words: "May the healthy not become sick,
and may the sick be healed."

The seventh day of the month of Mar Heshvan
arrived, and the rabbi's breath became light, his voice
could not be heard, he had lost the ability to speak; the
diphtheria was choking his throat. The doctors kept
on calming everyone, but those around the rabbi were
not calmed.

Yet the rabbi's joy kept increasing. After midnight,
he asked that his bed be moved to the large visitors'
room of the yeshiva. In that room were hung two plac-
ards honoring the generous donations of the *Bikkur
Holim* [the Visiting the Sick Society] of Chicago and
the *Hesed Shel Emet* [the True Kindness Society] of
St. Louis. The Hebrew expression *true kindness* means

kindness shown to the dead, which cannot be repaid. When his wife, the rebbetzin, saw where his glance fell, she burst out in a bitter cry. He turned to her and said with a smile, "Why weep? Now the real joy is beginning."

The students would not close their eyes to nap or rest; they would not even blink. They surrounded the rabbi's bed the whole night. Rabbi Meir requested paper and pencil and succeeded in writing in disjointed letters his final wish, "All of you drink '*L'hayim*'—'To life'!" The whiskey was poured into cups, and every student approached in turn to raise his cup and to bless the rabbi with "*L'hayim!*" The rabbi pressed his hand for a long time on each student's hand or shoulder.

The great teacher then told them all to dance, to dance with fervor, singing his famous composition "In You Our Ancestors Trusted; They Trusted and Were Saved." They danced in circles around his bed. On a small piece of note paper he wrote to them: "Only with joy!" The students touched his bed and danced with tremendous fervor, tears streaming from their eyes. The rabbi's face shone with supernal light; his whole being was flames of fire; all of him was joy; his trembling lips were whispering, "Only with joy! Only with joy!"

Suddenly, in the midst of this stormy dance, on an instant, the voice of the mighty song became silent. The great light went out. A cry of terrible dread burst from hundreds of students; it pierced through the great building of the Yeshiva Chochmei Lublin: "We're orphans; we've lost our father!"[26]

The Joy of Humor

ecause religion is the most serious aspect of life, there is always a danger of it becoming too serious, of it becoming heavy and severe. It needs to be lightened with the joy of holy humor.

In Judaism, religion and humor are not antithetical. A rabbi is even required to have a sense of humor, since the Talmud says that before a session of Torah study, a good teacher tells a joke to expand his pupils' minds. A talmudic story tells about Elijah the Prophet appearing in a vision to a mystic named Rabbi Beroka and, in a conversation with him, praising holy *badhanim*—comedians with a spiritual vocation to cheer up sad people—and saying that they would certainly have a share in the World to Come.

In recent centuries in Eastern Europe, more ordinary *badhanim* specialized in merrymaking at traditional Jewish celebrations, particularly weddings. A *badhan* would stand on a table at the feast and tell rhymed jokes—interweaving Torah or Talmud verses—making fun of prominent guests.

But in the period before the advent of the Baal Shem Tov, the Jewish people, suffering from terrible persecutions, were plunged into a profound sadness and were in danger of losing their collective sense of humor. The Baal Shem Tov taught them to laugh and smile again. He taught that there can be no true worship without joy, and his Hasidic movement revived not only religious singing and dancing, but also Jewish humor and laughter.

The Besht himself had an active sense of humor. It is said that he once made a humorous remark that brought smiles to the faces of the angels in the highest heaven. More than a few tales portray him as laughing broadly, sometimes without obvious cause. Humor had a natural place in his mysticism too, since jokes and laughter expand consciousness, the mystic goal. He once explained that a holy comedian or jester, like those mentioned in the Talmud, can, by befriending and cheering up a downcast person through jokes and humor, elevate him spiritually. Through humor and laughter for the sake of heaven, he said, you can elevate even your own childishness and raise it to spiritual heights.

The Besht elevated others through humor and elevated his own childishness too. He also knew when to laugh at the world. He once said, "Who is a holy jester? Someone who, when everyone is laughing at his piety, laughs at them, unconcerned at their mockery."

Rabbi Dov Ber of Mezritch, the Besht's great disciple, took the Talmud's recommendation of a joke before Torah study and applied it to prayer, so as to pray with a joyful expanded consciousness. Once, before daily prayers, he organized a practical joke on one of his Hasidim, and after everyone was convulsed in laughter, he called out, "Now let's pray!"[1]

The best humor is elevated and spiritual, but even lowly, foolish humor may be used to ward off sadness and depression. Rebbe Mendel of Yaroslav taught, "It is so important to avoid any sadness, even about your sins, that you should make yourself happy even by telling and listening to ordinary foolish jokes."[2]

According to the Kabbalah, all forms of pleasure derive from the bliss that emanates from the radiance of the *Shechinah* that shines through all the worlds. But that pleasure can be experienced on higher or lower planes. Rebbe Pinhas of Koretz, a great disciple of the Baal Shem Tov, once said that even the pleasure and laughter from a good joke come from the divine bliss that emanates from the *Shechinah*.

One of Hasidism's most appealing qualities is its sense of humor. Some Hasidic rebbes even had a *badhan*, a jester, of their own, as would a king at court, to lighten their burdens of office. A few of these *badhanim*, such as Rabbi Mordechai Rackover, the *badhan* of Rebbe Yaakov Yitzhak, the Seer of Lublin, became famous. The *badhanim* of great rebbes were not simple fools. They were usually rabbis themselves and spiritually advanced disciples of the rebbe. One of the Seer's greatest disciples, Rabbi Naftali of Ropshitz, who was renowned for his wit and wisdom, in his earlier years before he became a rebbe himself, sometimes performed as a *badhan* at weddings. Rabbi Mordechai Rackover and the Ropshitzer pursued humor as a spiritual path, as a way to God. Both of them appear in the tales in this section.

The Joy of a Wedding

◁◈▷ When they were younger, before they became famous Hasidic rebbes, the two holy brothers, Rabbi Elimelech of Lizensk and Rabbi Zusya of Hanipol, traveled around for a few years in "exile." This meant that they wore beggar's clothes and relied on others for food and shelter. They shared the "exile of the *Shechinah*," the Divine Presence, which is homeless in this world, so to speak.

In their travels, they came to the town of Linsk, whose rabbi was the great Rabbi Mendel of Linsk. His son, Rabbi Naftali, was a young man; he later became a great rebbe in Ropshitz and was famous for his holy sense of humor. When Rabbi Elimelech and Rabbi Zusya came to Linsk, they stayed at Rabbi Mendel's home, but though they were at the rabbi's Friday night Shabbat table, along with other guests, he totally ignored them; he did not even have them served food, and they had to eat some dry bread they had saved in their knapsack from the last meal they had eaten. They were surprised at this and thought that the rabbi had accidentally overlooked them. It was their holy custom, like some others who went into "exile," never to ask for food or anything else but to rely only on God; so they kept their silence. They thought it might be an oversight, but the same thing happened at the second Shabbat meal, Saturday midday. At the third meal, when it was dark, again they were not invited to eat, but they still went over to the table to hear the rabbi's Torah teaching. And they asked each other, "How come he doesn't notice us or pay any attention to us?"

At *havdalah,* they also came near the table to be close to the torch-candle and to make the blessing that God "creates the light of fire." After *havdalah,* Rabbi Naftali started to make rhyming jokes and was teasing them, saying, "Meilich, *freilich!*" [Elimelech, be happy!] and "Zusya, *kushya*" [Zusya, why do you have such a long face as if everything is so hard!]. Not everyone enjoys having fun poked at them, especially when they're hungry. Then Rabbi Mendel spoke directly to them for the first time, saying, "If I had walked around in exile, I'd look better spiritually than you do! You won't get anywhere by fasting and afflicting yourselves! You can accomplish more and fix more spiritually by eating and drinking than by fasting!" It was the practice of Rabbi Elimelech and Rabbi Zusya at that time to be severely ascetic, to fast often and physically mortify themselves.

Before they left on Saturday night, the rabbi gave them three coins, but since it was dark in the house, they could not see well. Later they saw that he had given them three one hundred-ruble coins. Rabbi Elimelech thought it was a mistake and wanted to go back and return the money. But Zusya said, "He wants us to serve God by eating. He probably intended that if we merited it, people would feed us without our asking—and we would then return the money—but if not, we should use the money to buy food as we travel." Rabbi Mendel did not feed them because he was displeased with their ascetic path and wanted to point out to them its deficiency. He wanted them to eat and enjoy life! How can a person rejoice in God if he is excessively ascetic!

After the rabbi's rebuke—that he would have accomplished more than they had if he had wandered in exile—they decided to continue with their exile for another year, which they did. But this time, they did not follow such a strict ascetic path. Rather, they kept away from possessions and materialism only so that eventually, when they conquered their desires, they could serve God through eating and so on.

After another year on the road, they concluded their exile. When they returned to Rabbi Mendel in Linsk after the year, he was so happy at the way they looked that he was clapping his hands and jumping up and down, saying, "That's what I wanted you to accomplish in exile!"

Some time later, Rabbi Mendel passed away. And his son, the young Rabbi Naftali, wanted to visit and spend time with the leader of the generation. Around that time, Rebbe Elimelech's fame as a great rebbe began to spread. Rabbi Naftali heard about him and wanted to visit him, but he was worried that he had embarrassed the two holy brothers with his jokes and perhaps Rebbe Elimelech still held this against him. But he decided to visit anyway, and if he had to apologize and humble himself, he would.

So he traveled to Lizensk. On Wednesday of the week, Rebbe Elimelech already knew by the holy spirit who was traveling to him and who would be visiting him for the Sabbath. So he said to his aide, "Rabbi Naftali is traveling here. When he arrives, don't let him in without telling me first." The next day, Rabbi Naftali arrived, and the aide went in to tell Rebbe Elimelech about his arrival while Rabbi Naftali stood outside the door. Rebbe Elimelech called out in a loud voice, "Is the son of the murderer here?" Rabbi Naftali's father, Rabbi Mendel, had refused them food when they were famished to show his disapproval of their asceticism. According to the Rabbis, someone who embarrasses another person so that the blood leaves his face and he turns white is considered as if he had spilled blood and murdered him. The father had denied Rebbe Elimelech food, and the son had humiliated him. But the truth is that Rebbe Elimelech really only wanted to humble the boisterous young man. So Rebbe Elimelech had his aide shut the door and would not let Rabbi Naftali enter. Hearing this sharp rebuke, Rabbi Naftali immediately fainted. Rebbe Elimelech gave his aide a bottle of whiskey, and he took it and he rubbed it on Rabbi Naftali's body to revive him.

When Rabbi Naftali returned to consciousness, he took the rest of the bottle of whiskey and went to the *beit midrash* to sit and drink! When there, he heard a big tumult, because there was a wedding of two orphans, a boy and girl, that was supposed to take place, but there was no money for the traditional gift of a *tallis* for the groom and no liquor or honey cake or the other items needed for a wedding, so the wedding could not take place. Rabbi Naftali ran out and went through the town collecting money for the *tallis* and for some liquor and honey cake and a little food to make a wedding. So he brought everything, gathered everybody together to the wedding hall, and conducted the whole wedding. Then he jumped up on the table and began some *badhanut,* some holy jestering, as customary. Everybody was very happy.

Meanwhile, Rebbe Elimelech was at home, expecting that Rabbi Naftali would return to him later, and he waited for Rabbi Naftali's arrival before his *minyan* began to say the evening prayers. When Rabbi Naftali did not come, Rebbe Elimelech tried to recite the evening prayers, but they did not go well. He felt some spiritual obstacle. He normally would have his evening meal after the prayers, but because he could not pray properly, he decided instead to first recite *Tikkun Hatzot,* the Midnight Lamentation over the destruction of the Temple and over all that is wrong in the world, because the *Shechinah* is in exile. But when he began, he saw that it too did not go well. "Why is this happening to me?" he thought. "I heard earlier that there's a wedding in town. Maybe the people at the wedding are doing something improper by engaging in mixed dancing or something else." Perhaps his prayers were not being accepted because he had not corrected some impious behavior in the town. So he sent his aide to the wedding hall to see what was happening and report back.

Meanwhile, Rabbi Naftali, to make fun and entertain everyone, had disguised himself as an old man with a long fake beard made of cotton, and he stood on the table telling jokes. When the aide arrived, he of course did not recognize Rabbi Naftali. But as soon as Rabbi Naftali saw the aide, he jumped down from the table, ran over to him, grabbed his hands, and began to dance wildly with him. The aide was startled, but Rabbi Naftali drew him into his joyous ecstasy until the aide's bones were melting with spiritual bliss. The aide did not want to go back to Rebbe Elimelech and report as he was supposed to.

While this was happening, Rebbe Elimelech began to wonder where his aide was and why he had not returned. So the rebbe himself went to see. When the aide saw through the window that the rebbe had come, he ran out and said, "Rebbe, don't go in! A madman is in there, and if you go in, he'll grab you and make you dance with him and it won't be befitting your dignity! Don't worry, I promise you, nothing wrong is happening inside!" So Rebbe Elimelech returned home and went to sleep.

The next morning, Rabbi Naftali, who was full of holy chutzpah, holy brazenness, went to see him, and without knocking or receiving permission to enter, he pushed open the door to Rabbi Elimelech's room. Upon entering the room, Rabbi Naftali said, "So what happened with your *Tikkun Hatzot* last night? Why did you have trouble reciting it?"

"Naftali, how do you know about my *Tikkun Hatzot*?" said the rebbe.

"Last night," said Rabbi Naftali, "both of us went to enter the heavenly palace. I was allowed in, but they didn't let you in. Why? Because the joy was so great at the wedding I conducted that they didn't want you to spoil it with your mourning!"

In Rebbe Elimelech's nightly recitation of *Tikkun Hatzot,* he mourned the *Shechinah*'s exile and separation from Her "Mate," the Holy One, blessed be He. But by uniting the bride and groom, with charity and then with dancing and laughter, the Ropshitzer was also able to unite the Heavenly Couple, the Holy One, blessed be He, and His *Shechinah.*

The task of kabbalists is to unite in marital union, so to speak, the two separated aspects of God, the Holy One, blessed be He [the "male" transcendent God] and the *Shechinah* [God in the world, the "female" immanent God]. The mystic truth is that there is not two but One. And in heaven, they preferred his way of holy joy to Rebbe Elimelech's holy sadness.

After this, Rebbe Elimelech drew Rabbi Naftali close to him, and Rabbi Naftali became the rebbe's intimate disciple. Although he had jokingly taught the rebbe a lesson, Rabbi Naftali still had much to learn from the holy Rebbe Elimelech of Lizensk.[3] ❧

Telling Jokes for the Sake of God

After the death of Rebbe Elimelech of Lizensk, Rebbe Yaakov Yitzhak, the Seer of Lublin, became his successor as the leader of Polish Hasidism. Rabbi Mordechai Rackover was a disciple and also the *badhan* of the holy Seer. And after Rebbe Elimelech's death, Rabbi Naftali of Ropshitz also became one of the Seer's greatest disciples. Like Rabbi Mordechai, Rabbi Naftali was very witty and sometimes also performed as a *badhan* at weddings. Appropriately, in this story, he defends his fellow disciple and *badhan,* Rabbi Mordechai Rackover. Since ordinary *badhanim* typically mixed Torah teachings and jokes, sometimes irreverently, some rabbis protested what they considered the "sacrilegious" performances of *badhanim* at wedding feasts. With some ordinary *badhanim,* such a charge might be true. But Rabbi Mordechai Rackover, the Seer's *badhan,* could not properly be suspected of disdaining holy things.

Rebbe Hayim of Chernovitz once traveled from the Ukraine to a wedding celebration in Poland at which the Seer of Lublin was also present. The Sabbath before the wedding, when Rebbe Hayim recited *kiddush,* the blessing over the cup of wine that precedes the meal, he was fervently turning and swaying this way and that, with wine splashing out of the cup in every direction! The Polish Hasidim were amazed; they had never seen anything like this! [The Chernovitzer was from an offshoot Ukrainian branch of Hasidism that had different customs from the main Polish branch. Although the Polish rebbes were also fervent in reciting *kiddush,* it was more "inward."]

Later, at the wedding feast, the Seer of Lublin's *badhan,* Rabbi Mordechai Rackover, jumped up on the table to entertain and started to imitate the Chernovitzer's recitation of *kiddush*. He was twisting and turning, the wine flying out of the cup. He did it perfectly, and everyone was hysterical. People were rolling on the floor laughing. Who was laughing the most? The Rebbe of Chernovitz! He had no idea of what he was doing or what he looked like when he was saying *kiddush;* he was in another world then. He said, "Where did he get this incredible routine from?" No one dared to tell him that the *badhan* was imitating him. But one *chutzpadik* [brazen] fellow did tell him. He said, "Rebbe, he's imitating you!"

On hearing this, the Chernovitzer felt humiliated: He was trying to serve God, and now he had been made a public laughingstock! He was too humble to blame the *badhan,* but nevertheless, when a tzaddik's feelings are hurt, there are consequences! The holy jester immediately became seriously ill, collapsed, and was taken into the *beit midrash.* He was actually dying.

They said to the Rebbe of Chernovitz, "Rebbe, forgive him! How can you let this happen to him?"

The Chernovitzer said, "How can *I* forgive him? This is not my doing. I have nothing against him. But he made fun of a Jew saying *kiddush* for God alone! He is being punished by Heaven, not by me!"

Rabbi Naftali of Ropshitz, who was very clever, was there and answered, "Rebbe, just as *you* recite *kiddush* for God alone, he tells jokes to make Jews happy, for God alone!" The Rebbe of Chernovitz raised his eyebrows. Was it possible? He had never heard of such a thing! The Ropshitzer said to him, "Rebbe, we'll make a test. If he's telling jokes until the last minute before he's leaving this world, we'll know he's doing it only to serve God."

So they went to the *beit midrash*. When they arrived, they found the holy jester lying on a bench, surrounded by his friends and the Holy Burial Society, who were caring for him in his last moments.

Now, in Yiddish, when you need to go to the bathroom, you say, "*Antshuldikt, ikh darf aroysgeyn*"– "Excuse me, I have to exit." Rabbi Mordechai was about to leave this world. As the Ropshitzer and the Chernovitzer stood there, they heard him, in his final minutes, when his soul was about to leave his body, joke to those around him, "Excuse me, I have to exit."

Hearing this, the Rebbe of Chernovitz looked over at the Ropshitzer and smiled from ear to ear. Then he laughed as he walked over to the holy *badhan*. He extended to him his hand, lifted him up, and, as he did so, Rabbi Mordechai was completely restored to health.[4] ⋙

As the Talmud teaches in the tale about Elijah the Prophet praising the two *badhanim* to Rabbi Beroka, making other people happy, making them laugh, is a great deed and a service of God. Bringing happiness to others is also a secret of being happy oneself. My rebbe, Rabbi Shlomo Carlebach, had a wonderful sense of humor. Shlomo used to say, "When you are sad and the gates of joy are closed, make someone else happy. Then, when the gates are open, you can slip in."

The Secret of Dying

When Rebbe Naftali of Ropshitz passed away, two of his top disciples—Rabbi Hayim of Tzanz and Rabbi Shalom of Kaminka, both of whom eventually became rebbes—went to seek another spiritual master. Since their rebbe, the Ropshitzer, had been a friend of the Belzer Rebbe, Rabbi Shalom, the "Prince of Peace" of Belz, they went to visit him.

After they had been in Belz a short while, the Belzer saw that they were very spiritually advanced young men. His custom was that when he judged that certain disciples were fit to receive esoteric mystic teachings, he revealed to them the secret of dying. Because you cannot live if you do not know how to die.

So he told them he wanted to reveal this secret to them. When they asked him how to prepare themselves to receive it, he instructed them to fast for three days and each night, after midnight, to go to the *mikveh* [ritual bath] and immerse eighteen times [in Hebrew numerology, eighteen stands for "life"]. After going to the *mikveh* on the third night, they should come to him. They did as he said, and on the third night, they went to the Belzer, and he whispered in their ears the secret of dying.

The next day, when they happened to be in the kitchen of the rebbe's house, they came upon the holy Rebbetzin Malka. Her husband had told her that he had revealed the secret to these two young men. She said to them, "What do you think of my husband, who can reveal to you such secrets?"

"We'll tell you," they said, "but first you have to remove all jealousy from your heart."

She went over to the corner and prayed, "Master of the world, please remove all jealousy from my heart!" Rebbetzin Malka was a great *tzaddeket*, a holy woman, whose status did not depend on her husband. Now, if you irritate a holy person, there are consequences, so they did not want her to be mad at them about what they would tell her. She came back and told them she had removed all jealousy from her heart and was ready to hear what they had to say.

They said to her, "Our holy master, the Ropshitzer, had already revealed the secret to us. We only wanted to see if it was the same as what your holy husband revealed. And it was. We want to tell you one more thing, but first you have to remove all anger from your heart." She went back to the corner, returned, and said, "I've removed all anger from my heart. Go ahead."

They said, "What a difference in the way our master the Ropshitzer revealed to us the secret of dying and the way your holy husband revealed the same secret! Your holy husband told us to fast for three days in a row and each night after midnight to immerse eighteen times in the *mikveh*.

"But listen to how the holy Ropshitzer revealed to us this secret. There was great poverty at the Ropshitzer's house. On the Sabbath, there was no meat or fish, only potatoes. Before the Sabbath, on Friday morning, the two of us had the job of peeling the potatoes for all those who would eat at the rebbe's table. We sat and peeled the potatoes and threw them into a large basin of water in front of us. But although the Ropshitzer's household was so poor, everything was on the level as it will be after the coming of the Messiah, with joy and laughter.

"On that Friday morning, as the two of us were in the kitchen peeling potatoes, the rebbe happened to pass by the doorway to the kitchen, and he looked in and saw us. He came in, went behind us, and stuck his head between ours, and with his arms around us, pushed all our three heads together. Then he grabbed one of the potatoes and *threw* it into the basin of water so that water splashed over all our faces!

"At that moment, we felt as if we had been immersed in the *mikveh* and been born anew. The rebbe then whispered in our ears the secret of death. And he walked out. But as he reached the door, he turned around to look at us and laughed: 'Ha, ha, ha!'"[5] ≅

There are two paths in Judaism: the path of love of God and the path of fear (awe) of God. A person can reach high spiritual levels by the path of fear, with holy sadness—about spiritual, not worldly, things—with fasting and asceticism; or he can reach high spiritual levels by the path of love, with holy joy and laughter, with singing and dancing, eating and drinking. Rebbe Simha Bunim of Pshis'cha once said to his disciples, "If one can reach God by eating or by not eating, why not eat?"

Both the path of joy and the path of sadness have their dangers: joy can degenerate into foolishness and indulgence, and sadness can cause depression, which prevents any spiritual progress. There is another danger in the ascetic path of fear of God. The Baal Shem Tov said that people who pursue a path of stern asceticism tend to become angry at their fellow humans; what could be worse? But love for God and joy in His service tend to make a person openhearted and loving to his fellow humans. So the best path is for a person to seek holy happiness in everything he does. That is the truer, more Hasidic path, the path of the Baal Shem Tov.

The Dancing Bear

The Rabbis teach that there is a mystical connection between Yom Kippur, the most solemn holiday of the year, and Purim, the most frivolous holiday. They say that the Hebrew *Yom Kippurim*—Day of Atonements, a variant of the more common name—means *Yom K'Purim,* "a day like Purim."

⋙ One Yom Kippur, before the blowing of the *shofar,* there was a serious heavenly accusation against the Jewish people, which the Baal Shem Tov was unable to nullify by his prayers. So he stayed in his private room and did not enter the synagogue for the *shofar* blowing. Sensing the gravity of the situation, his holy disciples sat in the synagogue in great fear and dread.

A simple Jewish villager, seeing the glum looks on their faces, ran home and came back dressed in the bear costume he wore on Purim, to lighten the mood and cheer everyone up. He cavorted and danced until he succeeded in making everyone laugh.

Immediately, the Baal Shem Tov entered for the *shofar* blowing and said, "The decree couldn't be nullified except by joy."

The anxiety of the Besht and his disciples prevented them from canceling the heavenly accusation

and judgment. Only when the spirit of joyous humor
passed through them was the decree nullified.

Later the Besht explained to his disciples what
had happened, commenting on the verse: "What, after
all, is joy?"[6] He said, "Even joy that is not from a high
and holy source, but merely foolishness of the category
'what after all?' or 'so what?'[7] makes an impression in
heaven."[8] ≈◈≈

The Power of Joy

≈◈≈ When Rabbi Simha Bunim of Pshis'cha was a
young man, he made a living for a period of time in the
lumber business. Every year, he traveled to the Danzig
Fair, where many merchants gathered, some selling and
some buying trees and lumber.

On one of these trips, when he was by the river in
Danzig, a terrible thing happened. A certain Jew slipped
and fell into the swift current of the surging river.
Another moment and he would drown. Everyone pan-
icked, and they were all crying out in terror, "Save him,
save him!" And they were all astonished to hear Rabbi
Bunim cry out to the drowning man, "Give my regards
to Leviathan"—the legendary giant fish!

The drowning man, who had lost hope of fighting
the current, heard him and suddenly began to struggle
again to save himself. Why? Because the rabbi's levity
snatched him out of his despair and aroused his will to
live. He finally found a floating plank that had been

cast out from a passing ship and held on to it until he was able to get back safely to shore.

There was a big crowd on the shore, but the man went straight to Rabbi Bunim and fell on his neck, saying, "You saved my life! If it wasn't for your clever words, I would have died because of my despair and the confusion I was in because of everyone's screams. But your joke aroused my will to live; because of you, I'm alive."

In later years, when Simha Bunim became a rebbe, he used to tell this story and conclude, "See the power of joy!"[9] ≈≈

Progress and Priorities

Joy, bliss, and ecstasy are the rewards of a life lived in the light of eternal truth. But the spiritual goals are love of God and love of fellow human beings.[1] If a person pursues love of God and people in tandem and focuses on faith, trust, and divine providence, he will certainly have his share of ecstatic joy.

More Important Than Ecstasy

Rebbe Yosef Yitzchok Schneersohn of Lubavitch told the following story.

≈≈ During the winter of 1913, when I was 33 years old, I went to visit my holy father [who was then the Lubavitcher Rebbe, Rabbi Sholom Dov Ber], in Menton, France. Menton is a seaside resort town. Every day he and I would walk together for hours along the seashore and talk. My father told me many awesome teachings and stories during these walks. He talked especially about meditating on

Hasidic concepts to prepare for prayer, while wearing *tallis* and *tefillin*. One day he was telling me about the awesome spiritual effect this kind of meditation has, describing it in numerous ways, saying, for example, that it causes light to descend from the higher realms to illumine the world and a person's soul. "This is true," he said, "of an ordinary person; how much more so of a tzaddik, for when a tzaddik meditates this way he experiences a divine bliss and delight and tastes the sweetness of God!"

"With God's help," said Rebbe Yosef Yitzchok, "I hope to always remember that glorious moment—the sight of my holy father's face flaring in ecstasy as he uttered the words, 'the sweetness of God.' At that moment, I felt I understood the words of his holy ancestor, Rebbe Shneur Zalman of Liadi [the first Lubavitcher Rebbe], who defined a tzaddik who attains the level of being a *merkavah,* a chariot of God, as someone who never ceases, all his life, even for a instant, from God-consciousness.

"Seeing my holy father strolling along the splendorous seashore, with its ocean waves and the strand of sand stretching ahead, yet immersed in godly delight and sweetness, I thought that he was certainly an *atzmi,* that is, a person who lives in God's presence every moment, a person of utmost spiritual integrity, who reveals the essence of his soul and acts identically regardless of who he is talking to or where he is—whether in a palace or a prison, whether talking to a prince or a pauper—even in the most beautiful natural surroundings conceivable, as now.

"For a long time after my father had said these words about the bliss and ecstasy of divine meditation before prayer, we walked together silently. I saw that everyone who passed us in the opposite direction stared at my father's face, because it was shining with a holy light. [His father was in a deep trance of *d'vekut,* in an ecstasy of God-consciousness.]

"Suddenly, as if he was waking up from sleep, my father turned to me and said, 'Yosef Yitzchok! I want you to know that the ecstasy a person gains from meditating before prayer, whether he is an ordinary person or even a tzaddik, is absolutely insignificant compared to what he gains if the Holy One, blessed be He, grants him only one thing: that he have a desire, an inclination to do a favor for another Jew, that another person be dearer to him than his own self. I tell you, it is worthwhile to toil hour after hour, day after day, toil of the body and toil of the spirit, to comprehend the divine, if the result is that one truly desires to do a Jew a favor!'"² ⊰⊱

Joy and ecstasy are important, but loving people is even more important. According to the late Rebbe Menachem Mendel Schneersohn, the son-in-law and successor as Lubavitcher Rebbe of Rebbe Yosef Yitzchok, the Baal Shem Tov loved all of creation and every one of God's creatures. The late Lubavitcher Rebbe taught that the Baal Shem Tov once said to a disciple, "I love my fellow Jews like my own self, but I love gentiles too. I feel love for every tree and plant and for every animal in the forest."³ Because of his love for the whole of creation, the Besht experienced transcendent joy.

In the Subway

I (Yitzhak Buxbaum) have had my share of experiences of mystic joy also. Many times when I was in the presence of my rebbe, Rabbi Shlomo Carlebach, we were all, under Shlomo's holy influence, ecstatically joyful.

Shlomo had a great sense of humor. Once, a group of us were together with Shlomo at his synagogue in Manhattan, and Shlomo was teaching. After a while, when we were bathing in joy, Shlomo jokingly remarked, "If the Messiah doesn't come now, it's his loss!"

If you were with Shlomo for a few hours, you would be ecstatic for a day. If you were with Shlomo for a day, you were ecstatic for a few days. If you were with Shlomo for a few days, you were ecstatic for a week. I used to think, "If I have this ecstatic joy by merely being in Shlomo's presence, where must his consciousness be?"

But I have tasted even higher levels of my own inner joy. When I was living in Jerusalem many years ago, there was a time when I was so joyful that, literally, no one could be within ten feet of me and not be happy. Why did I attain this great blessing then? One can never be certain, but I was living in the holy city of Jerusalem and pursuing my religious path. But it also related to the fact that I was working in Steimatsky's, an English-language Jerusalem bookstore—like many other non-Israeli Jews whose Hebrew was less than perfect and who could not get other jobs. In the bookstore, I was regularly given the chance to help and serve customers. Having always been a teacher, this was something new and precious. A teacher helps his students but at the same time can feel superior. I was spared that egotism when working at my humble job in the bookstore, and I derived the spiritual rewards from devoted service to my fellow human beings. I sat on a stool and waited for customers to enter, and I served them to the best of my ability. During that period of my life, I was brimming over with bliss; not like an idiot but with bliss and great joy. No one could be near me and not become very happy; people would break into smiles. That state lasted for about a month. May God grant me that experience again!

But not all experiences of mystic joy are so dramatic. When a couple fall in love, they become mad with their love: Everything is joy and bliss; it seems that the world is happy with them and around them. After they are married, they can try to keep the intensity of that peak time of their falling in love, but it is not always possible. A married couple may sometimes regain the romance they knew at the beginning of their relationship, but most of their lives together will be more prosaic—but no less meaningful. They develop a different kind of love that is very rewarding—an undercurrent of good feeling and shared happiness. It is that way too in the religious life, in one's relationship with God. When a person first becomes religious and falls in love with God, fireworks go off; there are great experiences. But they usually fade.

The Baal Shem Tov told a parable: "A man went into a candy store, and the shopkeeper let him taste a little bit of some of the candies. But when the customer wanted to continue tasting, the shopkeeper said to him, 'I gave you a taste so that you'd know how good everything is. But now you have to pay if you want more. I didn't treat you for nothing!'"[4]

The mystics say that God gives a person a taste of the sweetness of the Hidden Light;[5] God "lifts up the veil." But after that taste, he must "pay"; he must exert himself to achieve and earn that delight in the future, to make it a spiritual possession, to win mystic consciousness.

After tasting that joy at the beginning of his spiritual journey or later, a person with mystic aspirations tries his best to regain those exalted peak experiences and to make them a part of his normal existence. But whether he succeeds at that or not, if he perseveres, he will attain something less dramatic but still very meaningful: after years of effort at developing himself religiously, of working to establish a relationship with God, he will have a constant undercurrent of love and joy; he will even occasionally be rewarded with mystic experiences because of all the time and effort put in previously. And he strives for the highest always.

It is important to know that joy always accompanies love. We usually think of mystic awareness as expanded consciousness—a feeling of oneness and harmony—but an open heart is also a mystic experience; love is a revelation of God's presence. I learned this from my own experience and from reflecting on the life of my rebbe, Rabbi Shlomo Carlebach. Most of us have had occasions when our heart opened, when we were able to love someone. Shlomo's heart was always open to everyone he met. Cultivating an open heart is a sure path to mystic joy. I would like to tell a story of something that happened to me.

≈ Some years ago, I was teaching a weekly class on Jewish mysticism at night in a local synagogue in Queens, New York, and for a while was teaching about faith and trust in God. Faith is directly connected to mysticism; the Baal Shem Tov said that "faith is *d'vekut* [God-consciousness]." By cultivating and deepening one's faith, one makes God real in one's life and experiences God's presence. The Rabbis say that one of the ways to deepen your faith and trust in God is to study and immerse yourself in the subject. One important aspect of faith is the belief in divine providence, the awareness that everything happens by God's direction, that everything is meaningful and connected to everything else. So I had been reading many Hebrew books on faith in order to deepen my faith and was extracting useful quotes. I had a manuscript of them that may some day become a book. I was going to share some of the material from that manuscript with my mysticism class that night.

In the early afternoon that same day, I was also teaching a class on spiritual stories at the New School

University in Manhattan. While I was traveling on the subway from Queens to Manhattan for that class, I intended to work on my material on faith and trust, to prepare for the Jewish mysticism class that night.

When I got onto the train, the number 7 line that begins in Flushing, I noticed that it was rather hot. It was a hot day, and the car's air conditioner was on. But I saw that some windows above the seats opposite me were open, so the air conditioning was not working properly. It is part of my nature to be aware of the surrounding conditions—so I closed the windows in order for the air conditioning to work. A young man, who seemed to be a Russian Jew in his twenties, noticed this—I had closed the window above him—and I saw that he nodded approvingly at my efforts. When I was about to sit down, he pointed above my head; the window above me, I had not noticed, was also open. I closed it. He seemed to appreciate my doing all this.

A young Korean woman was also sitting opposite me on the other side of the car. I had closed the window above her too. She had an infant in one arm and was rummaging in her purse and something fell out on the floor at her feet. I thought she saw it, but when she did not pick it up, I motioned to her, and she nodded her head; she knew that something had fallen; a moment later, she picked it up. I thought, "How nice that I'm being helpful and communicating with people. That is the way it's supposed to be, because that is the meaning of life—to love and help other people."

A short time later, after the number 7 train had traveled aboveground for a while, I realized that the sun was coming through on the side of the train I was on. As it was becoming hot, I moved across to the other side and sat to the left of the Korean woman. I had spent ten or fifteen minutes reading my manuscript on faith, trust, and divine providence when I decided to give myself a break and looked up. I happened to notice a young black woman sitting to the right of the Korean woman, and my eyes fell on the magazine she was reading on her lap. It was open to an article titled "How to Want Only What You Already Have." I was struck by how closely related this was to what I was studying and took it as a sign from God supporting my attempt to immerse myself in thoughts of faith and divine providence. I was reminded of a Hasidic anecdote where a rebbe said, "I'm blessed that I never needed something until I already had it." According to the Jewish mystics, there are no coincidences; that I noticed she was reading something on a topic related to faith was providential.

I was thinking of making a friendly remark to her about this, but the Korean woman was between us, which made it slightly awkward, so I hesitated. But after a another minute, I leaned over and, catching her attention, asked her what magazine she was reading. She showed me it was the *Yoga Journal.* I told her that I was reading about faith and trust in God, and I told her about the Hasidic anecdote. She said in a nice way, "It's the same thing." I also felt good about this little exchange.

Again, I was relating to the people around me in a
friendly way, and one thing was leading to another.
When you become aware of divine providence, you realize that everything is connected, and if you are worthy
and your heart begins to open, the string that connects
the moments of God-awareness is love for other people.

I went back to reading the manuscript on faith
and was so immersed in it that I missed my stop at
74th Street and Roosevelt Avenue in Queens, where I
had to switch to the F train. I had to take another route,
so I continued on into Manhattan and got out at the
Fifth Avenue station, where I would also be able to
make a connection to the F train.

But after I had walked about thirty feet on the
platform, I heard a voice calling out, "Wait! Wait!"
I turned around and saw the young Russian Jewish
fellow running up to me. He said, "What were you
speaking to that black woman about?" I told him.

He then began to tell me—in poor English—that
his mother is very religious, although he is not. I asked
him his name; he began to say "Jan" and then said
"Yaakov." He then told me that two weeks earlier, he
had slept with a married woman and was suffering
emotionally from his wrongdoing! He did not know
what to do.

He told me that his mother, with whom he had
been living, had returned to Israel after two years in the
United States; they had moved from Russia to Israel and
then to America. She was lonely here, unemployed,
and upset that he was not as religious as she had wanted.

All their family was in Israel. He asked me to guide him
and give him some advice for what to do about his having slept with a married woman.

I told him the first thing that came to mind—
which, based on my knowledge of the ways of Hasidic
rebbes, I took to be inspired: I asked him if he had a
Book of Psalms in Russian at home. When he said yes,
I told him to sit down and just start at the beginning
and recite the psalms aloud. Every once in a while,
when he felt his heart opening a little, he should say,
"God, I'm sorry. What I did was wrong. I won't do it
again." He should recite the whole book of 150 psalms,
which is a traditional custom of piety and repentance;
it takes hours to complete.

I also told him that it seemed to me that what
he had done was because he was depressed about his
mother's leaving him. He had become disoriented and
had gone astray. He also missed his mother's love
and needed a woman's affection, so he did something
crazy. He thought for a moment and then said, "I think
you're right." I told him that he should begin to look
for a woman who would love him.

I embraced him on the subway platform and
wished him well. Then we each went our own way. I
realized later: Why did he speak to me? Because he saw
that I was religious person who was also open—a Jew
with a yarmulke who would start a conversation with
a black woman on a train. And why did God make me
miss my usual stop? So I would exit at his stop and
he could talk to me.

I switched to the F train and reached my station at 14th Street, near the New School. As I went up the stairs and was leaving the station, I came to the exit turnstiles and walked toward the middle one. I noticed that— strangely—all the others were open but this one said "No Exit," so I veered to the side to avoid it. But I saw out of the corner of my eye that a young woman was heading straight for it, so I told her, "It's 'No Exit.'" She thanked me in a nice way. Again, I thought, "That's the way it should be, people interacting in a kindly manner."

Again, one thing was providentially leading to another; things were connecting, and friendliness and openness were the themes; they were the string that held together the pearls of these encounters. All this had happened because of my study about faith, trust, and divine providence. Each event and interaction led to the next, and one thing was providentially connected to the other in a beautiful way. The Hasidic rebbes and mystics teach that by pursuing continuity in one's spiritual practice, one enters a deeper and deeper mood until the nature of one's experience changes. I had immersed myself in studying about faith, trust, and divine providence, and then things started to join, connect, and deepen. My heart was opening too.

I went upstairs from the subway onto the street. And in the three-block walk from the subway station to the New School, because of all these divinely connected events, I had entered into a mystic and ecstatic state of consciousness: My heart and eyes were now opened, and I saw many things. In that short walk, I saw all the colors and shapes of everything around me: every person's face, puppies in a window. I heard children's laughter and smiles. It was all serene and joyful, and everything took place in blissful slow motion.

When I arrived at my spiritual stories class, I told the students the story of what had just happened. I had previously told them a lot about my spiritual master, Rabbi Shlomo Carlebach—because knowing Shlomo had given me many insights into the stories we discussed in class. I told them that I felt that I had just had a taste of what it was like to be Shlomo, being truly open to the world, to God, and to people.

I told them that the Hasidic rebbes teach that the Torah promises a reward for some commandments of "length of days." Usually this is understood as an idiom meaning "long life." But the rebbes say it really means that when a person is truly religious, each of his days is very long, because it is full of so many real events, of encounters that touch the soul.

So many things happened while I was on the subway. A number of times in my life, I had had the privilege of walking on the street with Shlomo. When you walked down the street with Shlomo, he was running to everyone and everyone was running to him, because he was so open. People knew it and sensed it. A day like Shlomo's is so long. When you walked one block with Shlomo, you had more encounters and experiences than you would normally have in a week. We are surrounded by life; life is bubbling around us, but we are usually so closed off in our own shell that we do not experience it; we are not open to the beauty and the wonder of the world. But because of that subway ride, when I tuned in to faith and divine providence, I passed into a realm where I experienced a different reality.

During that spiritual stories class, I was inspired. The class was usually good, but this class seemed to have a completely spiritual atmosphere. One of the female students in the class had brought her boyfriend; she asked if he could come in, and I answered, Shlomo style, "How could he not?" At the end of the class, this young man, who was a sculptor, gave me a piece of his work as a gift. Why? Because I had given him something. This too was a providential continuation of a beautifully "long" day, another real encounter with a fellow human being.

As I left the building, I saw one of the female students standing outside. She usually dressed with style, and as I stopped to say hello, I jokingly complimented her, saying that she had won the "Best Dressed" award. She told me that she was studying fashion. We discussed how looking attractive gives something to others; it can make them feel better and improves their mood; it is art and pleases the eyes and mind.

As I walked past a certain bakery-café on Sixth Avenue on my way to the subway to return home, I looked as usual, admiringly, at the display of beautiful cakes and pastries in the window. I went in and told one of the workers that I always enjoyed seeing their beautiful display. He was so happy to hear it and said they took pride in making the display.

One thing led to another, and everything joined in the beauty of holiness. My heart had opened, and I was truly alive. I felt that day that I was touching in the smallest way what Shlomo experienced all the time. I felt that God was rewarding me for my efforts to deepen my faith. ◈

The Joy of a Holy Brother

Matthew Miller is a twenty-two-year-old college student and was a student of mine this past term, when I was again teaching my New School University course on spiritual stories. Matthew was a good, engaged student—humorous, boisterous, and intelligent. He often made profound and thoughtful comments during our class discussions.

Matthew is returning to Judaism, and in our conversations, I recommended to him a book of stories about my rebbe, Rabbi Shlomo Carlebach. Matthew chose to do his final paper for the course on that book, called *Holy Brother*. Shlomo always called everyone he met "Holy Brother" or "Holy Sister." The book is a collection of stories about people's encounters with Shlomo; it shows an awesome holy person—full of love for every human being—who lived in our time. Many people who read this book weep with joy. When I read it, I could not read more than ten pages without weeping from joy and having to put the book down until the next day.

When I received Matthew's final paper and began to read it, I smiled when I saw its cover sheet:

> *Holy Brother*
> Holy Brother Matthew Miller
> Holy Brother Yitzhak Buxbaum
> Holy Final Paper

This is how Matthew's paper begins:

⨠ This book has taught me more than probably my whole semester in school, if not more. When you were telling me to read it because it would change my life, I decided to get it. Your last comment was, "Matthew, if you don't have money to buy the book, pawn your shoes and run barefoot to the bookstore to get it!"

With that in mind, I went to the bookstore with my last $22.50. I was going to buy a cup of coffee first, but at the last minute I decided not to. As I was paying for the book, the total rang up to $22.40. Realizing that this would leave me no money for dinner or for a train ticket back home to White Plains, I was about to return the book to the shelf when I heard this voice ringing in my head: "Holy Brother Matthew, buy that book even if you have to pawn your shoes!" So I bought the book and later that night called a friend of mine who goes to another college in the city and asked him for a loan. I went to his dorm room and told him the story, and he loaned me five bucks in dimes and nickels and gave me some kosher chocolate cookies for dinner.

The next day back in White Plains, I took my dog for a walk in the park, and let him run around while I sat down on a bench and began my journey into the stories about Shlomo.

The first story that had a profound effect on me describes Shlomo in Berkeley in the early days of his career. In 1966, he went to perform at the Berkeley Folk Festival and was staying with a rabbi for the Sabbath. He asked the rabbi, if he found a few students hungry for spirituality, could he bring them back for the Friday night Sabbath meal? The rabbi said "Sure," and asked his wife to prepare a little extra food.

The way the festival was set up, all the performers were doing a little bit of their music at the very beginning, to give everyone a taste of what was to come. This was on a Friday during the afternoon. When Shlomo played and sang, he instantly had thousands of young people mesmerized. After he finished his ten-minute segment, he invited all the thousands of kids—"everyone who wanted to continue the experience"—to come for a Shabbat meal that night at the home of the rabbi, whose address he announced. Later that night, four hundreds kids came to the rabbi's house for the Sabbath meal!

It says in the book that Shlomo had "holy chutzpah," that is, holy arrogance and brazenness. First of all, just to get up and perform in front of people takes chutzpah; then to invite thousands of people and to bring four hundred of them back to the rabbi's house—without asking! That's holy chutzpah!

It seems that Shlomo knew what he was put here on earth to do, and he did not let anything stand in the way of his doing it. It is as if he did not have the normal limits that most people have. He had his own, different set of rules. He was so confident in what he was doing that he was not afraid of the world or of what people might think or say.

The only way to have such confidence in oneself and in one's purpose, I believe, is to truly know that a greater Being is directing and guiding and backing you.

Shlomo had such faith in God that he knew without a doubt that God was with him, and he also knew that he had a specific purpose in life and that he was capable of doing it. That is why he could bring four hundred non-religious Jewish students back to his host's home.

At times in my life when I felt strong and secure within myself, I have envisioned myself as a warrior of truth who could not be stopped. At other times, I felt completely guilty, as if everything I did was wrong. At those times, I would just try to be quiet and fade into the background, so that people would not complain, telling me that something I was doing was wrong. Shlomo knew that he was not wrong. He knew that he was innocent, that his intentions were pure, and that his holy chutzpah could be used to bring light and happiness to people.

After reading more and more stories like this about Shlomo, I began to feel inspired. Being a musician like Shlomo and having recently become religious, I could see how these stories could have a direct impact on me. I decided somewhere in my subconscious that I was going to see if his methods of rounding people up, to bring them light, were possible for me. I feel that people all want to throw themselves into something; they want to be led to happiness.

My band was playing a gig at Baruch College, for the Hillel Center. We play great exciting Jewish music. When I passed through the lobby of the building where the show would be, I saw hundreds of students milling around between classes. I thought to myself, "This is

going to be a great show, there are so many young people here!" I then took an elevator upstairs to the gig,
which was on the seventeenth floor.

When I got to the room the show would be in, I
discovered only a few Jews, maybe ten or twenty, in a
huge beautiful room filled with light, chairs, and good
food. Sad to say, the typical Jewish situation: all the
right facilities but not enough souls. We played a song
and then were told to stop so a speaker could speak;
we were asked to return in about fifteen minutes.

I said to my fellow band members, "There are
hundreds of kids in this school just milling around,
looking for something to do. Let's go get them!" Everyone agreed but had some excuse or other about why
we should not leave the area.

Something in me snapped, and I realized with the
inspiration of Shlomo's stories that nothing would happen if I did not make it happen. I was already feeling
energized, so I grabbed a hand drum and began running down the hallway singing a Hasidic melody. Some
of the guys supported me and followed, but others tried
to stop me, saying, "Are you crazy? You're going to get
us thrown out of here!"

I simply did not care. It made no sense to me that
there was the potential for something wonderful to happen upstairs and it was not going to happen because no
one knew how to get people up there. I realized it is just
that simple: Let's go get the people! I started running
through the building and singing at the top of my lungs.
I suddenly became even more energized—I was ecstatic

and full of supernatural joy—and was singing and calling out, "Come to the seventeenth floor! We're having an
awesome party!" Some of my band members were with
me and then other people started to follow behind,
singing along.

I made eye contact with everyone I saw. I went
over to every person I passed and shook their hand
warmly and gave them a personal invitation to our
party. I also wanted them to know that I was not crazy!
But I became more and more joyful and excited by what
I had had the courage to do. Before I knew it, I was running up to people I did not know and getting down on
my knees, begging them, "Please come, this is going to
be a great event upstairs!" I had learned at a workshop
once that there is a way to appeal for help, person to
person, soul to soul; that is what I was doing now. Most
of the students were Asian, black, or Hispanic, not Jewish; one student whom I invited said, "I'm Asian." I told
him, "That's OK—this is for everyone!"

I ran down floor after floor, singing and drumming
and begging people to come to the party. I finally made
it down to the first floor. I immediately went over to the
security guards and shook their hands and let them
know that I was OK, that I was not hurting anyone. They
did not complain or say a thing; they just smiled.

By that time, when I reached the first floor, we
had grown to a group of about twenty or thirty people
who were behind me and singing. Once in the lobby,
we continued singing Hasidic melodies and dancing
ecstatically in circles. Then I heard a lot of clapping

and, looking up, saw seventeen floors of people hanging over the banisters clapping—hundreds of people. The building is built with an empty space, an atrium, in the middle and you can see right up to the very top.

We charged back upstairs for a few flights, then took the elevator the rest of the way, and grabbed our instruments and started playing. Within the next five minutes, about two hundred people showed up at the room. The joy we all had—the music, the singing and dancing—simply cannot be described. ✎

Matthew's story is a great lesson about stories: that the point of religious stories is not just to enjoy them but to learn from them and do what the rebbes did. The joy that the rebbes and mystics experienced can be ours too.

The path of mystic joy still exists in Judaism. But as always, a person must seek in order to find. May we all find the path to God and to His divine bliss and eternal joy.

Notes

Introduction

1. 1 Chronicles 16:27. In the original verse, "His place" refers to the ancient Temple in Jerusalem.

2. *Ecclesiastes Rabbah* 6.

3. My discussion of the nature of joy has been influenced by the booklet *Mekor HaSimha* by the Breslov leader, Rabbi Schick of Brooklyn, and by the teachings of the Lubavitch Mitteler Rebbe as transmitted by Rabbi Shneur Zalman Stern of New Jersey.

4. "You must always be joyful and believe with complete faith that the Divine Presence is near you" (*Sefer Baal Shem Tov,* vol. 2, p. 202, no. 38).

5. The Baal Shem Tov taught, "It is essential to always be joyful, because without joy you cannot cleave to God, blessed be He, in *d'vekut* [devotional God-awareness]" (*Sefer Baal Shem Tov,* vol. 2, p. 202, no. 41). He also taught, "Joy is so great, because by joy a person can reach an exalted spiritual level where he sees the *Shechinah,* the Divine Presence" (*Sarei HaMaiya,* vol. 3, p. 168).

6. I heard this parable from Rabbi Shlomo Carlebach in the name of Rebbe Nachman of Bratzlav. I have retold it in my own words. I have never been able to find its written source.

7. *Genesis Rabbah* 68.

8. *Genesis Rabbah* 68.

9. *Kovetz Sippurim* (1959), p. 49, no. 13.

10. *Kuntres Hasidut: Ivdu Et HaShem B'Simha,* p. 41. Note that *they* is often used in rabbinic contexts as an indirect reference to God.

11. *Ohel HaRebbe,* p. 8, no. 12; Martin Buber (ed.), *Tales of the Hasidim,* vol. 1: *The Early Masters* (New York: Schocken Books, 1947), p. 315.

12. *Kovetz Tshuvot B'Inyanei Simha U'Vitahon BeHashem,* p. 18.

13. *BeHetzer Pnima,* vol. 1, p. 109.

14. *BeHetzer Pnima,* vol. 1, p. 109. The text mentions the assimilated Jews "of Chernovitz" because assimilated Jews of that time were referred to by the name of this town.

15. *Kuntres Hasidut: Ivdu Et HaShem B'Simha,* p. 33.

16. Ecclesiastes 3:4.

17. To understand the *Shulhan Aruch* and Rabbi Moshe's question, we must understand that according to Judaism, the ancient Temple was God's House on Earth and represented His presence among humanity. Its destruction and absence symbolize everything wrong with the world—all the injustice and cruelty, the lack of goodness and compassion. Therefore, the Code of Jewish Law states that a pious person should always anguish over the Temple's destruction and the departure of God's presence. Because God is, so to speak, "in exile" from this world, some pious Jews every night recite a special prayer service called the Midnight Lamentation to mourn the destruction of the Temple, the exile of the Jewish people from their land, and the exile of the Divine Presence. During this service, the pious also lament their own spiritual "exile," the personal failures and deficiencies that separate them from God.

18. The passage literally says, "The Sage already said that a person should have joy on his face and mourning in his heart." I forget which sage said this. It seems to be at variance with the

rest of the teaching, so I paraphrased in the text what I take to be the true meaning of the Seer's words.

19. *HaGaon HaKodesh Baal Yismah Moshe,* pp. 59–60.

20. *Hazon Ish (The Vision of a Man)* is in fact the title of a book written by this great teacher. Some rabbinic authors are referred to by the name of their most famous work, as here.

21. *Orchot Hasidecha,* p. 62.

22. This teaching is powerfully expressed, for example, in *Kuntres Hasidut: Ivdu Et HaShem B'Simha,* p. 57.

Rabbi Yisrael Baal Shem Tov

1. *Sefer HaToldot: Rabbi Yisrael Baal Shem Tov,* vol. 2, p. 631.

2. *Pe'ulat HaTzaddik,* vol. 1, p. 44.

3. *Arachin* 11.

4. *Ish HaPele,* p. 69.

5. *Keter Shem Tov,* p. 39. To clarify its meaning, I have translated the literal "to lift up holy sparks" as "to reveal the divinity of all reality."

6. *Reshimot Devarim,* vol. 3, p. 281, no. 12.

7. *Kovetz Sippurim* (1955), p. 31.

8. *Kol Sippurei Baal Shem Tov,* vol. 1, p. 207, quoting *Sippurei Baal Shem Tov.*

9. *Seder HaDorot MiTalmidei HaBaal Shem Tov,* p. 46.

10. *Be'er HaHasidut: Sefer HaBesht,* p. 186, no. 5. An interesting comment teaches that sadness is not decreed by God: "Sadness is not only bad for the soul, it is bad for the body, because it gives rise to many illnesses. People bring these troubles on themselves, for although every trouble is a heavenly decree—as the Talmud says, 'No one stubs his toe on earth below until it has been decreed first in heaven above'—nevertheless, sadness is not decreed in heaven. A person brings it on himself, and it is contemptible and hateful in the eyes of God. It is not

even proper for a person to become overly sad about his sins. When God decrees suffering on a person, He desires that the person receive them joyfully and in a cheerful spirit. How then is it possible that heaven should decree that someone should be sad?" (*Hedvat HeHayim*, vol. 1, *Osher V'Simha*, p. 236, quoting *Aderet Eliyahu*).

11. *Or Yesharim*, p. 139 (70a), no. 187; *Sippurei HaBesht* (Agnon), p. 32, quoting *Or Yesharim*; Buber, *Tales of the Hasidim*, vol. 1: *The Early Masters*, p. 70.

12. *Divrei David*, p. 66 (33a); *HaBaal Shem Tov U'Vnai Heichalo*, p. 139. The Besht taught that clouds symbolize mental confusion (*Sefer HaBaal Shem Tov*, vol. 1, p. 193, no. 171).

13. The term I have translated as *forgiven* literally means "whitened," as in Isaiah's verse about Israel's sins' being forgiven: if they were red as scarlet, they would become white like wool.

14. *Kovetz Sippurim* (1960–1961), p. 31, no. 31.

The Joy of Jewishness

1. *Kovetz Sippurim* (1954–1955), p. 31, no. 48. The blessing is literally "for not making me a gentile." Since this negative formulation would detract from the story for many people, I have expressed it otherwise.

2. *Hiddushei HaRaMaL* [Rabbi Moshe Leib of Sassov], Brooklyn (1991), II, p. 14, Parshat Bo and no. 51; *Devarim Areivim*, p. 30b, no. 1; *Ma'aseh HaShem HaShalem: Dinov*, vol. 1, p. 208, no. 8; *Likkutei RaMaL* [Rabbi Moshe Leib of Sassov], p. 8, Parshat Bo; Martin Buber (ed.), *Tales of the Hasidim*, vol. 2: *The Later Masters* (New York: Schocken Books, 1947), p. 83.

3. Heard orally from Rabbi Shlomo Carlebach. I have also used written versions of his telling in *Connections/Hakrev Ushma*, 1985, 1(5), 5; *Jewish Storytelling Newsletter*, Spring 1987, p. 1; Annette Labovitz, *Time for My Soul* (New York: Aronson, 1997), p. 395. A Hebrew version of this tale not from Rabbi Carlebach is found in *Sippurei HeHag: Pesah*, p. 110.

4. Adapted from a tale told by Rabbi Shlomo Carlebach. A written version of this tale, although not about the Bach, appears in *Oseh Felleh,* vol. 2, p. 401.

5. The kabbalists usually speak of four worlds. This lower world is the World of Action.

6. Micah 6:8.

7. The astronomy of Rebbe Nachman's day was of course not as advanced as that of modern times, but his point is made nonetheless.

8. *Sippurei Ma'asiyot,* p. 234; Aryeh Kaplan (trans.), *Rabbi Nachman's Stories* (New York: Breslov Research Institute, 1985), p. 447. I have adapted the text about the morning blessing. See note 1 about the Berditchever. The final quote is from Isaiah 64:3.

The Joy of Sabbaths and Holidays

1. *Netivot Shalom,* p. 287.

2. *Or HaTzafun,* II, p. 167. The quoted verse is Isaiah 58:13.

3. Today, because there is no Temple, there is no pilgrimage.

4. If you would like to know more about this glorious holiday, see my book *A Person Is Like a Tree: A Sourcebook for Tu BeShvat* (New York: Aronson, 2000).

5. *Sefer Baal Shem Tov,* vol. 1, p. 71, no. 83. Another source says that the Besht taught that one should decrease Torah study on Shabbat and concentrate on meditation (*yihudim*), so I added meditation here.

6. *Sefer HaBaal Shem Tov,* vol. 1, p. 71, nos. 85, 86; *Kovetz Eliyahu,* p. 115, no. 373; *Mazkeret Shem HaGedolim,* sec. 1.

7. *Funim Rebben's Hauf,* p. 91; *Connections/Hakrev Ushma,* 1985, 1(3), 2; *BeHetzer Pnima,* vol. 1, p. 148.

8. Heard from Rabbi Zalman Schachter-Shalomi at the Elat Chayyim Jewish Retreat Center, summer 1993. I also heard this from Rabbi Shlomo Carlebach. Hebrew versions are found in *P'ri Tzaddik Aitz Hayim,* pp. 166–174; *Imrot Tzaddikim,* p. 59, no. 1; *Yemot Olam,* p. 111.

9. *P'ri Kodesh Hillulim*, p. 80.

10. The text derives this teaching from the fact that the Hebrew *b'simha*, "with joy," is spelled with the same letters as *machshava*, "thought."

11. Literally, "May we all rejoice next year in Jerusalem, in a *sukkah* made from the skin of the Leviathan!" Jewish legend says that in messianic times, God will bring all Jews back to Israel and make for the righteous a *sukkah* from the skin of the giant fish, Leviathan.

12. *Beit Karlin-Stolin*, p. 182. That Rabbi Aharon Asher sang after every story and the effect his singing had on the listeners is found together with this story, but as a general description. I have included it at the end of this tale and added the detail about this taking place in the *sukkah*.

13. Based on Shlomo Majeski, *The Chassidic Approach to Joy* (Brooklyn: *Sichos* in English, n.d.), p. 88. The Lubavitch author, Rabbi Majeski, told me in a private conversation that he heard this tale from an old Hasid. In the form that Rabbi Majeski relates the tale, it is not stated explicitly, but the Berditcher seems to know what happened by the holy spirit. I've changed that miraculous element and said that the innkeeper told the rebbe.

14. *Otzar HeHag: Sukkot*, p. 286. A version told by Rabbi Menachem Mendel Schneersohn, the late Lubavitcher Rebbe, is found in *Kovetz Sippurim* (1968–1970), p. 2, no. 3; instead of the Ropshitzer Rebbe it is told about the Berditchever.

15. Deuteronomy 16:15–16.

16. *Sarei HaMaiya*, vol. 3, p. 168.

17. *Tehillah L'David*, p. 225, quoting A. Mordechai in the monthly *Beit Yaakov*, issue 44–45.

How Joy and Love Can Conquer Hate

1. Told by Rabbi Sam Intrator at the Purim feast, 1996, in the Carlebach Shul in New York City. Rabbi Intrator had heard this tale from

Rabbi Shlomo Carlebach. A written version from Rabbi Carlebach is found in *Leman Ahai V'Rayai,* p. 90. Another written version of this traditional Hasidic tale is found in Menahem Mendel, *Tiferet HeHag* (Jerusalem, 1991), p. 239.

2. This tale is based on a version in Moshe Prager, *Sparks of Glory* (Shengold, 1974), p. 78, and a version by Rabbi Shlomo Carlebach, in *Connections/Hakrev Ushma,* 1985, *1*(2), 3.

3. Based on *Gittin* 55b.

4. Heard from Rabbi Shlomo Carlebach and retold in my own words.

Portraits in the Ecstasy of Joy

1. *Toldot Kedushat Levi,* p. 16.

2. *Midor Dor,* vol. 3, no. 2253.

3. *Eser Orot,* p. 46, nos. 6–8.

4. Retold from a story heard from Rabbi Shlomo Carlebach. A written version can be found in *Shlomo's Stories* (New York: Aronson, 1994), p. 61.

5. Proverbs 5:19. The Hebrew word for "ravished" can also mean "err" and is used with that double meaning.

6. *No'am Elimelech,* p. 966, Igeret HaKodesh.

7. *Tzaddik Yesod Olam,* vol. 1, p. 168.

8. *Tzaddik Yesod Olam,* vol. 1, p. 65.

9. *Tzaddik Yesod Olam,* vol. 2, p. 59.

10. *Tzaddik Yesod Olam,* vol. 1, p. 228.

11. The famous Rebbe Nachman is popularly known as Rebbe Nachman of Bratzlav, but the Hasidim prefer the pronunciation "Breslov," which I use in referring to the sect.

12. Song of Songs 3:1–3.

13. Genesis 12:1.

14. *Sippurim Yerushalmiyim,* vol. 1; pp. 278, 280, 281.

15. *Sippurim Yerushalmiyim,* vol. 3, p. 105.

16. *Hayim Sh'Yesh Bahem*, p. 109.

17. *MiGedolei HeHasidut*, vol. 23, p. 40 (HaAdmor Rabbi Yeshaya Moskat MiPraga; HaAdmorim L'Veit Radzimin; HaRav HaGaon Rabbi Yitzhak HaCohen Feigenbaum); *Likkutei Aviv*, p. 265.

18. *Likkutei Aviv*, p. 265; *HaRebbe Rebbe Bunim MiPshis'cha*, vol. 1, p. 206, no. 6.

19. *Likkutei Aviv*, p. 267; *HaRebbe Rebbe Bunim MiPshis'cha*, vol. 1, p. 205, no. 5.

20. *Netivot Shalom*, p. 67.

21. One version of the tale says the rebbe was putting on Rabbeinu Tam *tefillin*.

22. *Sefer HaSichot* (1944), p. 9, no. 5. Another version of this tale is found in *Sefer HaSichot* (1942), p. 98, nos. 4–7. See also *Sefer HaSichot* (1940), p. 93, nos. 5–10.

23. Nehemiah 9:6.

24. This meaning is evident from a version of this tale in *Sefer Ha-Sichot* (1942), p. 98, nos. 4–7.

25. Compare what happened in the tale "Sabbath like the Chernovitzer." According to Rebbe Yosef Yitzchok Schneersohn of Lubavitch, the Hasidim of Reb Yekutiel's time did not particularly esteem him because he attained his spiritual levels partly through a blessing from the rebbe and not solely through his own spiritual efforts; *Sefer HaSichot* (1940), p. 93, no. 9.

26. *Ner Yisrael*, vol. 5, p. 99.

27. *HaHozeh MiLublin*, p. 265. I used a version that I heard from Rabbi Shlomo Carlebach for the ending of this tale.

How to Be Joyful

1. The *shofar*, a ram's horn, is traditionally blown on Rosh HaShanah and Yom Kippur.

2. *Kol Sippurei Baal Shem Tov*, vol. 1, p. 253, quoting *Sichot Yeka-rim*; see also *Kol Sippurei Baal Shem Tov*, vol. 3, p. 213; *Deva-*

rim Areivim, p. 7a, no. 19; *HaBaal Shem Tov: Ha'Ish V'Torato,* p. 259; *Seder HaDorot HaHadash,* section on Rabbi Meir of Premishlan; Buber, *Tales of the Hasidim,* vol. 1: *The Early Masters,* p. 80; *Aspaklaria HaMe'ira,* vol. 1, pp. 41–43; *Reshimot Devarim,* vol. 1, p. 6, no. 10.

3. *Kovetz Sippurim* (1968–1970), pp. 27–29, p. 28, n. 3; *Tanya,* chap. 22.

4. *MiDor Dor,* vol. 3, no. 1833. This anecdote is also found in *Netivot Emunah,* p. 158, about Rabbi Leib Hasid of Kelm.

5. Retold from a story heard from Rabbi Shlomo Carlebach.

6. *BeYishishim Hochmah,* p. 76.

7. *Yud-Gimel Orot,* vol. 2, p. 59.

8. *Hedvat HeHayim,* vol. 1: *Osher V'Simha,* p. 127. The text concludes: "In fact, he told them that if he had a shirt, he would not be happy because he would always be worried about needing to clean it and iron it and so on." I prefer the story without this sentence.

9. Based on *Hedvat HeHayim,* vol. 1: *Osher V'Simha,* p. 128, quoting *Darkei Musar.*

10. Paraphrased from *Netivot Shalom,* p. 311.

11. *Otzar HeHag: Sukkot,* p. 271.

12. The full text reads: "The *Gemara* (*Hagiga* 3) says, 'Why are infants brought [to the *hakhel* gathering where Torah is taught]? To reward those who bring them.' Now we learn in a *mishnah* (*Avot* 4:2): 'The reward of a *mitzvah* is a *mitzvah*.' The Rambam interprets this that the *mitzvah* itself is the reward. This is the meaning of 'to reward those who bring them.' Just like the infants, who come to pray, pray without any self-consciousness or posing and so on, the one who brings an infant merits to pray like an infant, without any posing or any pride or arrogance"; *BeYishishim Hochmah,* p. 298, no. 1.

13. The "holy sparks" represent the spiritual energy a religious person accumulates over many years of acting and yearning to

ascend spiritually; even ordinary Jews gather within themselves many such "sparks."

14. The *Midrash* is a collection of ancient rabbinic teachings on Bible verses.

15. *Tzav V'Zeiruz*, p. 18, no. 27. After conquering Jerusalem, King David brought the Ark to the city in a procession and danced before the Ark wildly, without caring what anyone thought.

16. Adapted from a story heard from Rabbi Shlomo Carlebach.

Dancing in Ecstasy

1. *Encyclopaedia Judaica*, vol. 5, "Dance," p. 1267. The quoted verse is Psalms 35:10.

2. Yitzhak Buxbaum, *Jewish Spiritual Practices* (New York: Aronson, 1990), pp. 487–488, quoting *HaNiggun V'HaRikkud Be-Hasidut*.

3. Buxbaum, *Jewish Spiritual Practices*, p. 489, quoting *Tiferet Maharal*, p. 10.

4. Buxbaum, *Jewish Spiritual Practices*, p. 483, quoting *Ish HaPele*, p. 75.

5. *Tiferet Banim Avotam*, p. 177.

6. *Otzar HeHag: Sukkot*, p. 284.

7. *Bas Ayin*, December 1996, p. 4.

8. *Shimusha Shel Torah*, p. 70; combined with *B'Ma'alot Kedoshim V'Tehorim*, pp. 28–29.

Lost in a World of Delight

1. *Avodat Avodah*, p. 289.

2. *Ma'aseh HaShem HaShalem*, vol. 3, p. 645, no. 17.

3. *Imrot Tzadikkim*, p. 7. The quoted verse is Proverbs 5:19.

4. The rebbe's words were especially hard to understand because this sort of remark was a motto of certain Jews who sought to make changes in traditional Judaism.

5. The weekly Torah portion is subdivided into seven parts. Lubavitcher Hasidim study one part each day of the week.

6. Y. Tauber, *Once upon a Chassid* (Brooklyn: Kehot 1994), pp. 26–27.

Eating in Ecstasy

1. Ezekiel 41:22.

2. *Kol Sippurei Baal Shem Tov*, vol. 4, p. 170.

3. Not to be confused with the legendary but related concept of the thirty-six hidden tzaddikim for whose sake the world exists.

Happiness Even While Suffering

1. Judges 5:31.

2. Based on *Rabbeinu HaKodesh MiShinova*, vol. 2, p. 303, with slight changes. The same story is told about Yehoshua Asher and his father, Rebbe Yaakov Yitzhak of Pshis'cha, the Holy Jew, in *Kedushat HaYehudi HaShalem*, p. 279.

3. *P'ri Tzaddik Aitz Hayim*, p. 137. Rabbi Shimshon of Uzriyan was the son of Rebbe Meshullam Feibush of Zabrizha. Rabbi Hayim of Chernovitz later became a rebbe. He appeared previously in the tale about his Sabbath ecstasy, "Sabbath like the Chernovitzer."

4. Psalms 34:9.

5. Psalms 105:2.

6. *Nifla'ot HaSaba Kadisha,* II, p. 80. The final sentence is mine.

7. Adapted from *The Holy Beggars' Gazette*, p. 43 (although without ascription, undoubtedly from Rabbi Shlomo Carlebach).

8. I have replaced a peculiar piece here: "Perhaps the hotel manager would murder him, out of fear of the lord, who gave the corpse over to him and locked him in there, because the lord would not believe that he was alive and would think that the manager had done something with the body." I replaced this with the more likely notion that having been murdered, he thought he might still be among his murderers.

9. *Kitvei Rabbi Yeshaya, Shohet U'Vodek,* p. 138, no. 15. The hymn "*Mah Yafit*" and a translation can be found in the Artscroll book *Zemiroth,* p. 102.

10. *Pe'ulat HaTzaddik,* vol. 1, p. 338, no. 601. I have omitted the end of this sentence, which reads: "because in the World to Come, one is even closer to Him, blessed be He." The meaning is unclear to me. Perhaps it means that since I am still close to my son and he is in the next world near God, I'm now closer to God.

11. Aryeh Kaplan, *Until the Mashiach: The Life of Rabbi Nachman* (New York: Breslov Research Institute, 1986), p. 184, says that the rebbe knew earlier that there would be a fire and had spoken about it at great length.

12. Derived from Psalms 91:15.

13. *Pe'ulat HaTzaddik,* vol. 2, p. 603, no. 918.

14. This paragraph is my own, inserted to explain what precedes it.

15. Job 2:4.

16. *Pe'ulat HaTzaddik,* vol. 2, p. 607, no. 923.

17. Job 19:26–27.

18. Based on *Sh'al Avicha V'Yagedcha,* vol. 1, p. 203.

19. Literally, "food cooked by non-Jews," the kosher status of which was uncertain.

20. Psalms 35:10.

21. Adapted from "A Torah Thought on the *Sedrah* of the Week," *Jewish Press,* October 20, 1989, and from English and Hebrew renderings: Rabbi S. Z. Kahana, *Legends of Israel* (Kabbalah Learning Center, 1996), p. 166; *Otzar HeHeg: Sukkot,* p. 162.

22. *Be'ero Shel Yitzhak,* p. 16, no. 3.

23. *Kol Sippurei Baal Shem Tov,* vol. 4, p. 227, quoting *Sippurei Hasidim.*

24. Or "She laughs at the time to come" (Proverbs 31:25).

25. *Shivhei HaRayah,* p. 26. Rabbi Yitzhak HaCohen Maggid was the great-grandfather of the first chief rabbi of Israel, Rabbi Avraham Yitzhak HaCohen Kook.

26. *Hedvat HeHayim,* vol. 1: *Osher V'Simha,* p. 61, quoting *Netzotzei Or HaMe'ir.*

The Joy of Humor

1. This is my own version of an anecdote recollected from Solomon Maimon's autobiography.

2. *Darkei Tzedek,* p. 21.

3. *Emet V'Yatziv,* vol. 3, p. 40, no. 2; another version of this story is found in *Hemdah Genuzah: Talmidei Besht, Gedolei Yisrael,* p. 56.

4. I originally heard this tale from Rabbi Shlomo Carlebach, who told me he had heard it from the Bobover Rebbe. My version is based on Shlomo's telling and on a written version of a telling of the tale by the Bobover Rebbe, found in *P'ri Tzaddik Aitz Hayim,* p. 134. The latter version has for the punch line "*Der oylam zol antshuldigen, di neshomo darf aroys!*" ("Please, everyone, excuse me, my soul has to exit!"). There is also a version of this tale in Rabbi Abraham Twersky's *Not Just Stories* (Brooklyn: Mesorah, 1997), p. 88. My version has previously been printed in Peninnah Schram (ed.), *Chosen Tales: Stories Told by Jewish Storytellers* (New York: Aronson, 1997), p. 66.

5. Adapted from a tale I heard from Rabbi Shlomo Carlebach. There are related written versions of this tale in *Imrot Tzaddikim,* p. 226, no. 6; *HaHochmah MaiAyin,* p. 148; and *Imrei Dvash,* p. 90.

6. Ecclesiastes 2:2.

7. The comment plays on the Hebrew in Ecclesiastes: *simha mah zo osah* and the phrase *mah b'kach,* meaning "nothing."

8. *Netivot Shalom,* p. 288.

9. *Hedvat HeHayim,* vol. 1: *Osher V'Simha,* p. 17.

Progress and Priorities

1. To learn more about love of people as a paramount goal of Jewish mysticism, see my book *An Open Heart: The Mystic Path of Loving People* (New York: Jewish Spirit, 1997).

2. *Once upon a Chassid,* p. 148.

3. Adapted from *Nezer HaBaal Shem Tov,* p. 70, no. 19-8.

4. Based on *Bas Ayin,* January 1995, quoting *Otzar Mishlei Hasidim; Midrash Rivash Tov,* II, p. 44, no. 1; p. 45, no. 2.

5. As noted earlier in the section "Portraits in the Ecstasy of Joy," the Torah says that God created light on the first day of creation but the sun only on the fourth day. The Rabbis say that the first light was the spiritual light. By it, Adam could see from one end of the world to the other. But God hid that light so that it would not be misused by wicked people. It is "reserved" for the use of the tzaddikim, the righteous.

Glossary

ARK The cabinet in a synagogue that contains the Torah scrolls, the holiest ritual objects in Judaism.

BAAL SHEM TOV Title by which Rabbi Yisrael, the founder of the Hasidic movement, is known, literally, "Master of the Good Name." The idiomatic Hebrew has two meanings: "a person who has a good reputation in the community" and "a righteous *baal shem,*" a kabbalistic faith healer who uses divine names to work miracles. Rabbi Yisrael was both a great teacher and a faith healer. See *Besht.*

BADHAN (PL., *BADHANIM*) Comedian; jester.

BADHANUT Holy comedy; jestering.

BEIT MIDRASH Torah study hall, often adjacent to a synagogue or serving also as a synagogue.

BESHT The Baal Shem Tov, from the acronym for the expression.

CHOLENT Traditional Sabbath meat and vegetable stew.

DAVVEN To pray the ordained Jewish prayers.

D'VEKUT God-consciousness; devotionally cleaving to the Divine Presence.

EREV SHABBAT Eve of the Sabbath; Friday during the day.

FOUR SPECIES   *Etrog* (citron), *lulav* (palm), *hadasim* (myrtle branches), and *aravot* (willows) ritually waved on Sukkot.

GAON   Great Torah scholar; genius.

GEHINNOM   Hell.

HAGGADAH   Text of the story of the Jews' exodus from Egypt, recited on Passover.

HAKAFOT   Dancing in circles while carrying the Torah scrolls in the synagogue on Simhat Torah.

HASID (PL., *HASIDIM*)   Member of the Hasidic movement; literally, "a pious person."

HASIDISM   Jewish pietistic movement that originated in Eastern Europe in the eighteenth century. Many Hasidic sects are named after the town where they originated, such as Lubavitch, Ger, Boyan, Breslov (Bratzlav), and Karlin (all mentioned in this book).

HAVDALAH   End-of-Sabbath ceremony that marks the transition from sacred time to profane time.

HAVURAH   Group of people who join together to perform specific *mitzvot* or other good deeds.

HUPPAH   Bridal canopy.

KABBALAH   The teachings of Jewish mysticism.

KADDISH   Mourner's prayer.

KAVVANOT   Kabbalistic formulas; intentions.

KIDDUSH   Sanctification; blessing recited by the man of the house over wine before the first two Sabbath meals (Friday night and Saturday midday). If there is no wine, the blessing may be recited over bread.

KITTEL   White robe worn on Passover and Yom Kippur.

KOL NIDREI   "All Vows"; Yom Kippur prayer that annuls all vows.

MAGGID   Preacher; teller of sacred tales.

MEGILLAH   Scroll; in particular, the scroll of the Book of Esther, read aloud on Purim.

MIDRASH   Collection of ancient rabbinic commentaries on the Torah.

MIKVEH   Ritual bath.

MINYAN   Prayer quorum of ten Jewish males.

MITZVAH (PL., *MITZVOT*)   Divine commandment derived from the Torah. Traditional Judaism is based on a system of *mitzvot*.

MUSAR   Non-Hasidic pietistic movement that focuses on perfection of character and ethics.

NE'ILAH   Final prayer of Yom Kippur, "Closing of the Gates," last chance for prayers to be received.

NIGGUN (PL., *NIGGUNIM*)   Hasidic melody, often wordless.

PASSOVER   Holiday commemorating the Jews' exodus from slavery in Egypt.

PAYOT   Earlocks.

PESACH   Passover.

PURIM   Holiday celebrating the Jews' being saved from extermination in ancient Persia.

RASHI   Great rabbi and scriptural commentator.

REB   Honorific, equivalent to *Mr.*, used with a man's given name.

REBBE   Hasidic sect leader, also called a *tzaddik;* teacher. A rebbe is always a rabbi, but most rabbis are not rebbes. A rebbe usually has many rabbis among his followers, although most of his followers are ordinary Jews. All those who accept his leadership are called his *Hasidim.*

REBBETZIN   Wife of a rabbi.

ROSH HASHANAH   Jewish new year holiday.

SABBATH MEALS   Three Sabbath meals are eaten: after the Friday night service, after the Saturday morning service, and on Saturday in the late afternoon, after the afternoon synagogue service. Sabbath meals are generally eaten at home, but Hasidic men eat the third meal in the synagogue with the rebbe.

SEDER   Ritual meal celebrating Passover, during which the *Haggadah* is recited.

SEDER USHPIZIN   "Order of the Holy Guests"; recitation welcoming the mystic appearance of seven guests in a *sukkah* on Sukkot: Abraham, Isaac, Jacob, Moses, Aaron, David, and Joseph.

SELIHOT   Penitential prayers for the week leading into Rosh HaShanah.

SHABBAT   Sabbath. The Jewish Sabbath begins at sundown Friday night, when the woman of the house lights Sabbath candles in the home, and lasts until sundown Saturday. There are three Sabbath prayer services in the synagogue: Friday night, Saturday morning, and Saturday afternoon.

SHAVUOT   Festival of Weeks; holiday commemorating the giving of the Torah to the Jewish people at Mount Sinai.

SHECHINAH   Indwelling Divine Presence; "female" immanent God.

SHEHECHEYANU   Blessing recited for having reached an "auspicious time."

SHIVA   Seven days of most intensive mourning for a deceased.

SHOFAR   Ram's horn blown on Rosh HaShanah and Yom Kippur.

SIDDUR   Prayer book.

SIMHA   Joy; by extension, a family celebration.

SIMHAT TORAH   Joy of the Torah; holiday when congregants dance with the Torah scrolls.

SUKKAH   Temporary booth used for eating, living, and even sleeping during Sukkot.

SUKKOT   Festival of Booths; holiday commemorating the ancient Jews' having survived the exodus from Egypt, when they lived in temporary dwellings (booths) in the Sinai Desert.

TALLIS   Prayer shawl.

TEFILLIN   Phylacteries; little leather boxes containing scriptural verses handwritten on parchment that men wear strapped to their head and arm while reciting the morning prayers. They symbolize a person's being bound to God and having his mind and heart directed to God continually.

TIKKUN HATZOT Kabbalistic Midnight Lamentation Service, mourning the destruction of the ancient Temple and the exile of the Divine Presence from the world.

TORAH Jewish scripture; the Five Books of Moses; literally, "teaching," "instruction."

TU BESHVAT New Year of the Trees; holiday ordained by the kabbalists, observed by eating fruits.

TZADDIK (PL., *TZADDIKIM*) Literally, "righteous person"; applied to a saintly or holy person or a Hasidic sect leader or rebbe.

YESHIVA Academy.

YOM KIPPUR Day of Atonement; the holiest day of the Jewish religious calendar.

The Author

YITZHAK BUXBAUM is an inspired and inspiring storyteller and teacher, one of those reviving the honorable calling of the *maggid* (preacher), who in times past traveled from community to community, awakening Jews to the beauty of their tradition. The author of the highly acclaimed *Jewish Spiritual Practices*, called "the best book written on Jewish spirituality," Mr. Buxbaum has also written *Storytelling and Spirituality in Judaism*, *The Life and Teachings of Hillel*, and other titles. He teaches at the New School in NYC, where he resides, while lecturing and performing at synagogues, JCCs, and retreats throughout the United States and Canada. Mr. Buxbaum has a Web site at www.jewishspirit.com.